RAILWAY
KILLER

The lonesome clatter of the freight train rattling through the night, its horn blaring, evokes great feelings of inner security among residents of most railway towns.

Those sounds perfectly sum up the immense distances of the vast nation of America and man's efforts to conquer them.

But, in the summer of 1999, for hundreds of thousands of people whose homes skirted railway tracks across America, that familiar sound came to mean something else. The sound of fear. The sound of evil. The sound of death.

For somewhere on the vast railway network was a cold-blooded killer, a man whom the FBI believed had murdered many innocent souls. He had been riding the rails for more than 20 years, drifting across America from Miami to St Louis to Los Angeles. Then the urge to destroy people's lives turned him into a homicidal maniac.

THE
RAILWAY
KILLER

WENSLEY CLARKSON

JOHN BLAKE

Published by John Blake Publishing Ltd,
3 Bramber Court, 2 Bramber Road,
London W14 9PB, England

www.blake.co.uk

First published in paperback in 2007

ISBN: 978-1-84454-323-6

British Library Cataloguing-in-Publication Data:

A catalogue record for this book is available from
the British Library.

Design by www.envydesign.co.uk

Printed and bound in Great Britain by Bookmarque Ltd, Croydon

1 3 5 7 9 10 8 6 4 2

Papers used by John Blake Publishing are natural, recyclable
products made from wood grown in sustainable forests.
The manufacturing processes conform to the environmental
regulations of the country of origin.

Every attempt has been made to contact the relevant copyright-
holders, but some were unobtainable. We would be grateful if
the appropriate people could contact us.

To all those who have lost their lives at the hands of serial murderers.

The US–Mexico border is the next frontier
of American consciousness

Author Carlos Fuentes

an American to Mexicans
a Mexican to Americans
a handy token
sliding back and forth
between the fringes of both worlds ...

– Excerpt from *'Legal Alien'* by Pat Mora

Author's Note

Angel Resendez, the man whose life and crimes are described in this book, shares one important criminal characteristic with Andrew Cunanan, killer of Gianni Versace and four others in 1997; they both fit the commonly used definition of 'spree killer' because they were engaged in the business of killing one person after another.

'Spree killers are a type of serial killer involved on a full-time basis in their killings and in running from the law,' says James Alan Fox, dean of the College of Criminal Justice at Northeastern University, USA.

However, Resendez is unique because he continued travelling back to his family between many of the slayings he allegedly committed. Cunanan did not.

This puts Angel Resendez on a criminal pedestal from which he earned the titled 'America's Most Wanted Man' during the hot, early summer months of 1999.

Resendez changed his name frequently during his adult life. In an effort to avoid confusion, throughout this book he is referred to by his birth name Angel Resendez.

Also it is worth noting that some of the dialogue represented in this book was constructed from available documents, some was drawn from interviews given at the time of his arrest, and some was reconstituted from the memory of participants.

Prologue

The leafy streets of the university district on the edge of Lexington, Kentucky, USA, assumed an eerie calm after dusk. The tall buildings of the nearby college channelled a cutting wind south from the flatlands beyond the city boundaries, causing anyone out after dark to hunch their shoulders against the breeze.

For more than a hundred years, that wall of night-time silence had been interrupted only by the sound of freight trains shunting slowly along the street-level tracks that ran beside a quiet residential road littered with neat one-storey homes and a handful of apartment blocks.

On the steamy night of 29 August 1997, a small, shuffling figure sprang from one of those passing trains and landed on the grass verge alongside the rail line. He quickly recovered his balance, picked up his sports bag and dusted down his jacket and jeans with leathery palms as he had done hundreds of times before.

Then he turned towards a line of homes just a few yards to his right and stood looking across at them intently. There were lights on in all of them and he wondered which was the one he needed to visit.

The cars of the two-mile-long freight train were still slowly creaking along the tracks beside him. But he paid little attention because he was so used to the railway. It had long since become the key to his life – and survival.

As the last car passed, he glanced up and watched the back of it moving through the misty night, occasionally illuminated by the streetlights alongside the track and the strong, clear moon in the blotchy black and grey sky. Gauze-thin clouds scudded across the night, momentarily blocking out the stars.

Meanwhile, the train picked up speed as it drifted off into the distance.

Just then, the slightly built man heard a noise to his left that had nothing to do with the train. It sounded like two people talking. He ducked down behind a bush at the side of the tracks and waited. He had an idea...

~

On that same night, Christopher Maier, 22, and his girlfriend had been to a party held by friends from the University of Kentucky, where they all studied.

They'd decided to head over to another student party and were walking along the side of the same main track that ran along the edge of the university campus. It was late, but neither of them felt it was unsafe as they had walked along the same route many times before. In any case, the street was well illuminated and the district was far from rundown.

Suddenly, Maier's girlfriend stopped walking. 'What was that?'

'Excuse me?'

'Didn't you hear something?'

Maier shook his head and tried to walk on.

'I think someone's over there,' she said, pointing towards a clump of bushes a few yards ahead.

Maier smiled, shook his head and grabbed her by the hand. They continued walking.

~

Under the influence of the alcohol and drugs he'd just consumed in the empty freight train car, the man hiding behind those bushes was now beginning to come down from his drug-induced stupor. The euphoric rushes he'd been travelling with were leaving him, replaced by an edgy, nervous anxiety, which could only be relieved with more drugs.

He was shaking while he crouched behind that bush as the young couple got closer and closer.

His dark eyes searched the night; looking for anyone else who might be close by. He knew what he wanted, he just needed to be certain there were no witnesses.

The man remained crouched there for a minute longer as he collected his thoughts. He looked up one last time to make sure no one was watching.

When he was satisfied he was unobserved – he had a

sixth sense about such things – he leaped out from behind the bush and confronted the young couple.

He had what appeared to be a knife in his hand and immediately stuck it into Maier's side. 'Gimme your money,' said the man, with a Spanish accent.

'We don't have any,' responded the couple.

The man exploded with anger and virtually spat out numerous obscene profanities. He ordered the couple to sit down next to the bushes and pulled out some rope he had in his gym bag.

The couple were terrified. They did everything he told them to do and prayed he would not harm them. Maier even pleaded with the man, 'I'll go get you some money. You can have my car. Anything. Please, just don't hurt my girlfriend.'

But Maier's brave response simply angered the man even more.

They could see the hatred in his eyes flaring by the millisecond. The girl then looked across in horror as she saw the man strike her boyfriend on the head with a blunt object. As it plunged into his skull, it made a soft, crushing noise. Maier tried to fight him off, but it was impossible to find the strength as the man smashed him over the head again and again. Maier's body shook violently. He was choking and gagging on his own blood.

The last living image she had of her boyfriend way his glazed eyes staring helplessly towards her. She knew at that moment he was gone.

The man calmly let Maier's body crumble to the

ground. Then he looked over at the girl and moved towards her.

She pleaded with the man to help Maier. For a moment, he even stopped in his tracks and went back to examine the student he'd just bludgeoned to death. He looked down at Maier's lifeless body lying on the dusty ground and then glanced over the girl. 'You don't have to worry about him no more.'

He moved to the girl and began punching her in the face. Harder and harder. He broke her jaw and eye socket and cut her head and neck with the rings on his knuckles. The attack was so relentless that the girl eventually passed out. Then he raped her viciously. He dragged her limp remains over to the bushes and tore down branches, which he used to cover her body and that of her boyfriend.

Then he turned and walked away, satisfied that he had just left the dead bodies of two people by the side of the railway tracks.

Minutes later, the killer hopped on another train as it shunted through Lexington. He knew that, by the time police found the corpses, he'd probably be safely back south and close to the Mexican border where he belonged.

Back under those bushes, the girl eventually recovered consciousness. Terrified that her assailant might still be there, she was at first too scared to move. She knew that he had left her for dead. Eventually, she fought off the branches that had been so carefully laid over her body.

Although she did not know it at the time, that young student was the only living witness to the vicious killings committed with such venom and hatred by a man who would later become known as the 'Railway Killer'.

1

The locomotive's whistle at dirt-road crossings was a familiar sound to the residents of Puebla, a city with a population of well over a million, nestled in a valley between a clutch of Mexico's most fearsome-looking volcanoes. The local train service still used steam engines back in the late 1950s, and clouds of sweet-smelling smoke would waft across the town at regular intervals after the main express chugged through the dusty streets.

Its old cranking engine would clatter and clunk on narrow-gauge iron rails, drumming a sturdy, steady beat as its great pistons strained their way up to the city on a plateau more than 2,000 feet above sea level. Alongside the rusting hulk, many of the town's barefoot kids would scramble to get a look inside the long line of cars in its wake.

Often boys as young as four or five would jump into

the cars to try and steal some fruit or vegetables, before leaping to safety when the train picked up speed as it exited the town.

This was the world into which Angel Leoncio Reyes Resendez was born on 1 August 1959.

~

Virginia Reyes Resendez, a pretty, young mother-of-two, hurried out into the humid summer heat from her tiny one-bedroom shack on the edge of Izucar de Matamoros – one of Puebla's hillside slums – to a relative's rusting wreck of a VW Beetle. She was extremely worried. The pains in her stomach indicated that her pregnancy might be about to end prematurely. She wanted to have the baby like her other two. But life never seemed to go smoothly for Virginia. Here she was, pregnant at 25 and already abandoned by the child's father, Juan Reyes. She wasn't surprised he'd fled because he was penniless and incapable of resisting the lure of alcohol.

But Virginia was determined to make sure this child was born healthy. She had never forgotten how a local priest invited into the family shack by a relative had predicted that her third child would be a boy who would possess great intelligence that would help Virginia and her loved ones escape the slums forever. The priest said, 'One day a boy will come and illuminate your life and make you very famous.'

At the time, she had taken little notice of the priest's kind words, but, as she was being driven along a bumpy dirt road towards the local medical centre, she began to once more hear his words ringing in her ears.

To Virginia – ever the daydreamer – marriage had at first seemed to offer the route to happiness for a woman who had felt her destiny was to remain on the poverty line forever. Virginia's marriage five years earlier had actually provided nothing more than a brief respite from the drudgery and poverty of life in a slum where running water and plumbing was a rarity. Virginia's family saw the marriage as an ideal way to get her off their hands. In their eyes, she was a maternal young girl who had struggled at what little schooling she received. Marriage was the only answer for her survival. In Virginia's eyes, she was a child who always played second fiddle to a bottle of booze or a slap in the face.

As usual, Virginia's happiness had been short-lived. Her husband had struggled to find work in Puebla as he drifted around the crowded streets. One day he left the family home to try and get manual work across the border where many of his friends had earned good money working for the *gringos*. He never returned.

So it was that Virginia had worked as a cleaner in a pizza parlour; slaving at gruelling double shifts to try and keep the family fed. It was only after her husband had gone that she found out she was pregnant for a third time. Now the strain of life was threatening to turn her latest pregnancy into a disaster.

The day before Virginia went into labour, she cleaned their tiny home from top to bottom. In many ways it helped her avoid thinking about her desperate situation: often alone, about to become a mother for the third time when she could barely afford to feed one child on the $10 a week her husband occasionally sent in from his travels. Virginia's pride prevented her from asking for money from relatives. In any case, most of them were just as poor as she was. However, she was determined to survive with or without her runaway husband's help.

As her relative's rusting VW Beetle charged through the crowded streets of Puebla, Virginia felt no fear. But then she had no choice.

The medical centre they finally arrived at was only marginally more hygienic than her shack of a home. As she was helped through to the maternity ward, the sheer numbers of other women about to give birth seemed overwhelming. Many of them were screaming and some of them were actually giving birth in the open ward as dozens of others looked on.

Half an hour later, Virginia was the one giving birth. 'It's a boy,' announced the doctor, holding up the tiny infant with his mop of black hair. 'What are you going to call him?'

Virginia looked up bleary-eyed, and forced a smile as she looked in the direction of the beautiful, neat features of the infant. 'He looks like an angel.'

One of the nurses smiled. 'What a beautiful name.'

'Yes,' replied Virginia, remembering what that priest had told her. 'He is a gift from God and his name is Angel.'

The truth was that Virginia had not given her newborn son's name much thought. She had felt it a bad omen just in case there had been complications.

But, as Virginia lay there recovering from the birth of her son, she felt detached from everything that had just occurred. It was as if those dramatic events had happened to someone else. She was worried about the welfare of her other children back at their rundown home, with no one there to look after them.

Virginia could not even afford to register the birth of Angel, although she was obliged by law to do so immediately. The doctor's medical fees were paid with coins collected from some cousins and friends who lived in the neighbourhood. It wasn't until weeks later that Virginia scraped together the $1 birth registration fee and – because the family wanted to avoid being fined for failing to register the birth earlier – they declared that Angel had been born some days later. Even at birth, the need to reinvent family history had become a necessity.

But there was nothing that unusual about this. More than a quarter of a million births every year in Mexico are not registered at all.

From then on, Angel celebrated two birthdays every year. As far as his family were concerned, it was on 1 August. Officially, it was some weeks later.

But, back in 1959, Virginia had no time for postnatal depression. She breastfed Angel whenever possible for many months because it was the natural, cost-effective way. By the time she left the hospital, with her tiny

Angel wrapped in a blanket in her arms, she had already worked out a game plan. The child was going to be her inspiration. He would be something special. That priest and his predictions might just turn out to be true.

Soon after the birth, Virginia got another job serving behind the counter of a luncheonette, working up to 12 hours a day for just over a dollar a day. She would leave little Angel in the care of her sister who lived in the same street in Izucar de Matamoros. Virginia had to make work her priority if they were to survive financially. She would drop her baby son at her sister's even more dilapidated shack across the dusty pathway from her home, then take the bus into work every morning. Angel would not see his mother again until the early evening.

Not surprisingly, Virginia felt enormous guilt over having to leave her children with relatives while she went out to work. However, she steadfastly refused to rely on anyone for support.

On her return to the family home each evening, Virginia would change nappies, cook supper and then fall asleep. Her only entertainment going to a friend's house once a week where she would lap up the corny dialogue and appalling storylines of the Mexican soap operas that dominated evening viewing on the local TV station. Her friend was about the only person for miles around with a television.

'It was not a real existence,' Virginia explained. 'I had few friends. My life was wrapped around the children and work when I should have been out having a good time with my husband.'

Virginia's addiction to the cheesy Latino soaps was her only release. Years later, she scraped together the money to buy a TV and then she would sit and watch them for hours on end. The men seemed so handsome and honourable. Why couldn't *she* find a man who was the perfect combination of these TV characters?

Angel, his mother, brother and sister all grew up together as one family unit. 'It was them against the world,' one relative later explained. But they all desperately wanted to find an escape from the poverty and degradation. Even back in those days, it seemed that the United States of America was the place where all their dreams belonged.

Virginia often thought back to the friendly priest who had made those bold predictions about her third child. Maybe the answer to her problems lay in that infant. Certainly, when she looked at the beaming child, he gave her a feeling of optimism and she believed he might be the key to her happiness. He seemed truly to be an angel sent down from the heavens.

2

The road where Angel was raised was typical of the dusty, rock-covered sheets of the Puebla slum areas. It had a bar, a primary school, a Catholic church and dozens of rusting, burned-out old cars. The older women tended to sit in the sun on the steps outside their shanty homes. Children would be constantly kicking footballs around.

The slums sprang up because a fifth of Mexico's population of 200 million people were living in 'absolute poverty'. In a country where the minimum wage even as it entered the new millennium was still only $120 a month and the cost of renting an apartment in any big city was at least $450 a month, it is no surprise that a large percentage of the population ends up in self-built properties about the size of a small garage.

Many of the slums, such as the one where Angel was brought up, were built on to hillsides because it was easier for the non-existent plumbing to drain off. Many of the kids played football during the day because they couldn't afford to do anything else. Many didn't even learn to read or write.

Angel's family would often find themselves looking across to the better parts of Puebla and its sprawling suburbs, dreaming of what life must be like with such luxuries as carpeting, sanitary systems, cars and, most important of all, money.

Sixteen of Angel's relatives lived at one time or another in or near the place his family called home. It was a messy plot of land with three small shack homes. Written in black paint across a strip of wood was the supposed street number. A paper sign taped to the stone gatepost announced: 'KITES FOR SALE'.

And, when strangers appeared, the boys playing street football would stop kicking and gather round them in the hopes of scrounging a coin.

For the first few years of his life, Angel shared a bed with his mother and sister. Angel was scared of the dark and would start crying unless the lamp was left on in the house's only bedroom. His mother would wait until he was fast asleep before climbing in beside him. It wasn't until he reached the age of five that Angel slept on a rotting mattress on the floor of the living-area with his older brother.

Their home was simply furnished. There was no telephone, no fridge and no proper plumbing, although eventually they did get an electric socket for a light.

When you're born into poverty, any toy can provide

a vital means of escape from reality. In the shack where Angel grew up, he had a teddy bear but little else.

There was no garden to play in, but near by there was a rough piece of hillside where he and the other kids would play football. Although the game became a comfort in the daytime, it never replaced his beloved teddy bear in his bed.

Angel was an awkward, slightly built child. His teeth protruded so much that it was often difficult to hear what he said. He also gave the impression to the other kids that he was a bit slow. In fact, he was just painfully shy.

Angel's cousins and his older brother were an important influence on his life. They often defended him when he was taunted by other kids. His name and small size meant he received more than his fair share of bullying from other kids. Often, Angel would be the last player to be picked for any makeshift football side because he looked so unimpressive. He never forgot that humiliation and promised himself he would prove them wrong and would race around the football field the moment a game started, chasing everything that moved – but he wasn't very good at it.

Besides football, Angel was fascinated by bullfighting and used to regularly try and sneak into the local arena. The first thing that struck the young Angel was that it was such a rusting mess, just a huge expanse of concrete with a roof on it. More important, there were the foot-long hot dogs for sale at dozens of rusty sidewalk stands.

The young Angel never forgot some of the bizarre and grisly sights that greeted him as he watched the matador slowly extinguish the life of the bull while a vast crowd cheered on. He was fascinated by the colour of the bull's blood as it seeped on to the sand-covered floor of the ring.

Sometimes Angel would take a drum with him that he beat incessantly throughout the contest. Men all around him would be swigging from bottles of cheap *cerveza* as they shouted insults that ranged from disparaging remarks about the matador's mother to the condition of the bull.

Angel was transfixed by what he saw. The matadors were supposed to be the heroes, but sometimes he would will the bulls to get their revenge. He watched with fascination when the matador was caught in the animal's horns and tossed into the air.

Death seemed to be a sport. It didn't look so bad. So why were so many people in fear of it?

~

Puebla's history spoke volumes about its attitudes towards the not-so-fortunate. Back on 5 May 1862, local soldiers inflicted an overwhelming loss on French invaders led by Napoleon III. And, ever since, Puebla has retained a reputation as a city not to meddle in.

All around Angel were vast Spanish colonial buildings plus the ubiquitous strong influence of the Catholic Church dating back to the time of Cortes. In fact, the Catholic Church was probably the only thing that all of Puebla's residents – rich and poor – had in common. At Easter time, they would all meet either at the Cathedral of the Immaculate Conception, the Church of La Compania or the Church of Santo Domingo. On such occasions, it was not unusual for more than 100,000 of the city's population to turn out in the *Zocalo* or main square.

The Church played a vital role in the lives of Puebla's poorer and destitute. Some saw it as a means of escape from the appalling poverty, while others considered the Church as an essential religious experience.

In the case of Angel's family, Catholicism wasn't a round-the-clock preoccupation, but it definitely influenced their lives. Virginia was an extremely religious person and would try to get to church at least once a day.

Angel was immersed in all this religion from an early age. As he grew older, he came to accept that his mother and other relatives needed Catholicism to get them through their difficult lives. But Angel sometimes found it difficult to equate their own poverty with the existence of a God. 'Why doesn't he help us?' he would ask his mother. She never knew how to reply.

Puebla's slums had a reputation as a dangerous breeding ground for young criminals and drug dealers for as long as anyone could remember. The uncertainty of life in the slums meant that kids had to learn quickly how to survive. Some even reckoned an assassin could be hired for $100 in one of the area's many bars without much effort.

The harsh reality was that the residents of the slums didn't care about yesterday because it was irrelevant, and they certainly didn't worry about tomorrow because it might never come. Many were drawn to crime or quick thrills like drugs, sex or alcohol. It was a lethal combination.

Even the police, overworked and undermanned, would stand by helpless. And sometimes they even joined in, taking bribes and kickbacks or venting their macho spleens by using street kids like Angel and his companions for target practice.

On many occasions armed police would raid the street where Angel lived. They'd drag alleged drug dealers out on to the dusty track and beat them with rifle butts. On one occasion, according to locals, a 16-year-old dealer was dragged away by three officers and taken to the back of a nearby police station where a vat of acid was kept. The officers then took bets on how quickly the teenager would dissolve.

Being a slum kid also meant being the subject of appalling humiliation from more fortunate people. At Puebla's only takeaway restaurant, rich kids in expensive cars liked to drive slowly round the parking lot, tossing French fries out of the window and watching the street children scratch and claw each other in a battle to eat the tiny morsels of food.

It would have been difficult for Angel not to sink into criminality like so many other young boys in the slums. His mother tried to protect him, but she was out at work most days. Virginia was an honest, hardworking woman and it was an unwritten rule in her household that, while no one volunteered to pay any taxes, you should never rob one of your own.

At first Virginia was slow to acknowledge that her son Angel was going to end up in trouble. She dreamed of a full school education for him, followed by college and a safe, responsible well-paid job. She believed that the priest's prophecy must have referred to that kind of success.

But Angel had already caught the crime bug. At every available moment, he would be out on the dusty streets, stealing melons from backyards or swiping cans of food from the grocery store.

By the age of six, he was in demand as a supplier of cheap fruit to local street sellers. He might have been small and wiry, but he didn't stand out in a crowd and that made him an effective petty thief.

On weekends, Angel and some of his friends began jumping trains into the city centre and heading for the busiest shopping areas. Thousands of kids regularly made the same trip to try and make some cash. It was a precarious journey that involved clinging on to the side of the cars as the train swept through the city streets.

As one boy who was brought up in a similar slum area explained, 'The kids back in those days had nothing – no computer games and videos to go home to. So they went to the rich areas and tried to develop their skills as thieves in the hope that one day they'd escape the poverty.'

So it was that Angel and his young friends stole,

scrounged and begged to survive. Angel soon realised he was only ever happy when he had some money in his pocket, and he knew he needed to get himself into a position to make a lot of money.

Even as a young child, a life of crime was *that* important to Angel.

3

At school, Angel would have had few problems learning the basic reading and writing skills except there were so many diversions outside the classroom that his education suffered. Also, he was a bit of a dreamer whose fantasies were filled with visions of living in a huge expensive *casa* with a big car.

Those dreams drove him straight towards Puebla city centre and that life of crime. Often, he'd skip school for days on end to join older kids thieving and scrounging on the busy streets.

Obviously, his mother Virginia didn't want Angel to turn to a life of crime, but she was powerless to stop him. And there was no man in the house to lay down the law. She feared for her son's future, but at the same time she had to continue the struggle to survive.

And Angel did not exactly cut an impressive figure. As one of his relatives later explained, 'Angel was timid and reserved. He was almost frightened. It seemed as if the only way he could express himself was by stealing something.'

Angel was playing truant so much that Virginia often had to walk him to school and wait by the gates for at least an hour each morning to make sure her wayward son did not try to leave the premises.

Angel simply changed tactics, waiting until the first school break and then disappearing, usually to the city centre where he'd start thieving as usual. On a number of occasions, he'd even spot his mother and dash through a back gate to avoid being caught.

When Angel did actually attend classes he impressed his teachers with his fast mind and ability to memorise things. They couldn't help wondering how good he would have been if he'd bothered to attend school more often.

However, Angel's physical development was extremely stunted. He was weak and ill-looking much of the time and at least two or three inches shorter than most of his friends.

Drugs were already being used by many of the kids in the shanty towns, where glue-sniffing was especially popular. And the lust for such substances often led to slum kids being lured into an even more twisted world – prostitution. Small, skinny Angel with his dark, vulnerable eyes would have been a prime candidate for the meat rack if he'd looked a few years older.

~

Shortly after Angel's sixth birthday, the little boy's

already troubled life was shattered by the news that his beloved mother Virginia was going to marry another man.

His name was Luis Maturino and he'd already clashed with Angel and his brother and sister when he had tried to discipline them following a problem with a neighbouring family. As a result, there was a feeling of mutual animosity between the children and their new stepfather-to-be.

The atmosphere inside the tiny shack where all of them lived was so bad that Virginia begged her brother Rafael Rasendez-Ramirez to let Angel live with him because she didn't want to upset her new husband. Uncle Rafael farmed a strip of land and owned a grocery stall in the local market, so he was, relatively speaking, one of the 'richer' relatives.

Being rejected by his mum was a devastating blow to the street urchin whose only vein of stability had been Virginia.

As Rafael later explained, 'Angel refused to go to school any more. He kept disappearing for days on end and then coming home when he was hungry. There was nothing I could do to stop him.'

The only light at the end of the tunnel for young Angel at this time was his grandmother who lived in the dusty countryside north of Pueblo. After being abandoned by his mother, he formed a close bond with his grandmother, but the long distance to her home meant that, as he got older, the journey took less and less of a priority in his life.

It's easy to blame Angel's absent father for his life of crime at such an early age. If his parents had stayed together, maybe they would have found the money to be able to keep him off the streets. On the other hand, it might have made absolutely no difference.

~

When the 1970 World Cup football tournament came to Mexico, Angel and all the slum kids were gripped by football fever. Even the slums became drowned in white-and-green Mexican flags.

Angel, his cousin and a handful of friends chose the only house on the street with a TV set to watch host nation Mexico's progress in the tournament. The Mexico team was strongly favoured to do well, but, when they were knocked out in the quarter-finals, Angel burst into tears as the final whistle was blown. The boys wandered home in a depressed daze. In Mexican terms, it was a national disaster.

But at least it provided a happy memory for the ten-year-old. And there certainly were not many of those at that time.

4

Eighty miles from Mexico City, Puebla, even years ago, was one of the most important bustling centres of industry, business, culture and finance in the entire Mexican nation.

Those who lived on the right side of the tracks in Puebla were among the most affluent and influential in Mexico. But, for the poverty-stricken peasants who flocked to Puebla in the hope of finding work, it was just another dirt-ridden city where only the strong survived.

As Angel grew older, he became more and more interested in the trains that came rattling through Puebla at all times of the day and night. Soon he was hopping on the ledge of open cars for a long-distance ride. Sometimes he'd spend two days aboard what was one of North America's longest and highest steam railways, built in the late nineteenth century as part of a rail network designed specifically to haul gold, silver, coal and timber.

That slow journey would take young Angel along mountain edges past old Hispanic farming towns, tatty water towers and rotting railway sidings. As the train gained altitude, it would creak almost to the point where it sounded as if it were about to split in two. The long procession of cars would rise gradually from the high plains to mountain forest, before the train would curve back on itself and pass through an aspen grove suffused with yellow light. Flat-stemmed leaves would flutter in the breeze.

On that train, he could breathe in clean, cool fresh air and dream of getting away from the grime and misery.

Back in Puebla, when he wasn't out thieving or wandering the streets, Angel was curious about his surroundings. Sometimes he'd sneak into the city's only library, but his reading abilities were so limited that what his mind demanded – knowledge – could not be sufficiently fed thanks to his poor education. It was extremely frustrating.

With his brown eyes and jet-black hair, Angel looked like dozens of the other kids who searched for scraps and hopped the trains as they chugged slowly through the slum towns on the edge of Puebla.

He remained slightly built and skinny, but then his daily caloric intake was barely enough to feed a small dog. However, his ability to smile warmly at strangers and look completely harmless served him well in the local markets and stores where he often stole food and clothes for himself and his family.

~

Angel's family struggled on in Puebla with barely enough money to eat one square meal a day. Then it was announced that the German car manufacturer, Volkswagen, was planning to build a massive plant on the edge of the city to produce its hugely successful Volkswagen Beetle automobile.

There were stories in the local press that the company wanted to employ upward of 10,000 local people. In a city where unemployment among the working classes ran at more than 50 percent this was a golden opportunity.

The only other businesses that employed more than a handful of workers was a ceramic the factory and a plant where sickly sweet potatoes, called 'Camotes', were churned out at a rate of 10,000 a day.

But no one in Angel's family ended up getting one of those 'dream' jobs at the VW plant and their life on the poverty line continued.

~

In the spring of 1972, Angel – then 12 – walked out of his uncle's two-room shack for the last time.

Rafael said, 'I never heard from him again.'

He simply presumed that Angel had taken off with a few friends to hop a freight train and head for the US. The need for work and money was the only driving force for a kid like Angel.

He'd become increasingly estranged from his mother and even his beloved grandmother. There was nothing left holding him back from his dreams.

But Angel did not immediately take the high road to the US as he knew that he looked too young to get any decent work. Instead, he fell in with a group of slightly older street boys and they formed a pick-pocketing and burglary gang on the side of Puebla opposite to where his family lived.

The gang was quite successful and Angel found himself leading a better lifestyle than he had back with his various family members.

And, once armed with some cash, Angel even tried to mend bridges with his mother by seeing her once or twice a month. But then she compounded his unhappiness by announcing she was moving with her new husband to the city of Ciudad Juarez near the US border.

Angel remained on speaking terms with his mother, but he never entirely trusted her. He felt he'd been betrayed once too often, and he would never let that happen again.

Meanwhile, Angel and his gang slept most nights out in the fields. However, one or two of the older boys would disappear at night into the city centre where they'd offer themselves for sex to older men in the narrow streets off the main square area of Puebla.

They told the younger kids in the gang that they got a good bed in a hotel for the night and got paid for the privilege. The fact they had to perform intimate, painful sex acts with complete strangers seemed a small sacrifice to make.

But then Angel and his friends had little or no understanding of morals, health and even the basic difference between right and wrong. Their lives had been such a struggle for so long that simply to survive was an achievement. Stealing from others and selling your body to the highest bidder was purely a means to an end.

However at only five feet in height; Angel was still considered too small to be taken along on the streets hustling for sex with strangers: The older boys knew the police would be more likely to target them if they were seen around the city centre with young kids.

But they told Angel his turn would come eventually.

~

One afternoon out by a small river on the edge of the fields where they so often slept, two of the older gang leaders sexually molested Angel after stripping him naked.

His family would later claim it was an experience that cast a dark shadow over his entire life.

Angel was so devastated that, when he next saw his mother on a rare visit to Ciudad Juarez, he broke down in tears and told her what had happened.

Virginia later recalled, 'When he told me, he cried a lot. I did not know what to tell him. The only thing I could say was that Christ loved him.'

Angel told his mother in the hope that, by sharing the full horror of what had happened, it might bring them closer together. But his mother had no idea how to deal with the assault. In a place like Puebla, there was no question of calling the police because of the shame that it would bring upon the family.

Angel later said he hoped she would at least try to seek revenge on the perpetrators. She just simply referred it all to God. And that confused Angel even further.

It took more than 25 years before Virginia would conclude, 'I failed him as a mother.'

~

Virginia tried in her own way to compensate for having abandoned her son for more than six years by making him feel as welcome as possible whenever he visited her tiny rundown home in the shanty town on the edge of Ciudad Juarez.

But Angel found it difficult to communicate with her as he grew older. He remained loyal to her in public, but beneath the surface he didn't trust her an inch. He could see through all her guilt.

Virginia was as penniless as everyone else around her, but whenever she got back from working across the border she tried to link up with her wayward son. And she was always buying him gifts to try to win his affection.

Meanwhile, his stepfather remained a distant figure, rarely even bothering to greet Angel when he appeared at his mother's doorstep.

Angel's reconciliation with his mother should have marked a happy turning point in his life. At least, he now had one parent to look up to. But he saw it in an entirely different way, as he later told a friend. 'She could never mend the pain and unhappiness. She was trying to buy my love, but it was already too late,' explained Angel.

~

By the age of 13, he'd already spent more than a year out on the road, fending for himself most of the time, and he'd concluded, not so surprisingly, that he didn't need the care and affection of anyone in order to survive.

He had managed to teach himself to read by avidly poring over newspapers he found in rubbish bins in the street. He even joked with his gang friends that he was the only one completely free to do what he wanted. That meant drinking alcohol and popping pills. But he could only dream about having sex with any girl who took his fancy, as – following that sexual assault by those older boys when he was 12 – Angel had become even more shy with girls. He was no more than five-feet-five-inches tall, and he felt vulnerable when he met girls who were taller than him.

After that attack by those older boys, Angel decided he had to get completely away from Mexico and begin a new life. He didn't want to settle any place in particular. He just wanted to be on the move, away from the perverts, the cops and his sick and twisted friends who had abused and then deserted him.

So he headed for those familiar railway tracks that had remained just about the only consistent image throughout his childhood.

5

Ciudad Juarez – with its Spanish colonial buildings and the constant wind whistling across from the nearby Rio Grande – is located in the vast Mexican state of Chihuahua, just across the US border from El Paso, Texas. The city itself was considerably smaller than Puebla, with a population of around 700,000, but, because of its close proximity to the US, that figure fluctuated enormously depending on the time of year.

At night, Juarez turned into a den of vice with transvestite nightclubs, prostitutes on every dimly lit street corner and cheap booze available to anyone with a dollar to spare.

But literally hundreds of thousands of residents moved across the border to work each year at harvest time. Mexico was – and still is – an important source of cheap, often illegal labour. Some believe that, if Mexico permanently closed its borders with the US tomorrow, the world's most powerful nation would fall into economic disarray rather than the other way round.

Not surprisingly, Ciudad Juarez boasted an extensive railway system with more than 3,000 miles of track connecting the entire state of Chihuahua with the US border and across to the modern Mexican port of Topolobamp. The state of Chihuahua had seven border crossing points with the US, three of them linking Juarez with El Paso.

Ciudad Juarez was also the first stop in young Angel's attempt to start a new life when he went to visit his mother at her new home. He knew that she would be in touch with some people who'd have advice about how to get into America. Angel had become almost obsessed with gathering knowledge about the place that so many Mexicans referred to as 'the promised land'.

He met Mexicans who talked in glowing terms about the riches of the US and the ease with which local people could make that crossing into the wealthiest nation on earth.

Many of the locals made the most of the opportunities provided by living in both countries. Numerous residents would make sure all their children were born on the US side because citizenship gave them access to education and healthcare benefits. On the other hand, they could take advantage of the low cost of living in Mexico, while enjoying some of the goods and luxuries of the US.

And, when illegal immigrants went across the border to buy groceries and clothes in one of the huge

American supermarkets, it was only natural to bribe the Mexican customs officials on their return across the border. Most of Ciudad Juarez's residents – rich and poor – believed that their quality of life was improved by purchasing what they could afford in the US.

Angel listened to all this talk avidly and somewhat jealously. He felt many of the people in Ciudad Juarez were too Americanised, although what he heard about certain aspects of life in the US made it a very attractive proposition to a penniless teenager without a proper home.

Angel discovered from many of the locals who illegally entered the US from Ciudad Juarez that the best places to slip across the border unnoticed were by two bridges – the San Jeronimo-Santa Teresa, and the Anapra-Sunland Park.

So, at the age of 14, Angel decided to find out what the United States of America was really like.

~

The biggest problem with the US–Mexican border has always been that no one is really in sole charge of its jurisdiction.

The bridges between the two countries are particularly badly managed. Customs, Immigration, the FBI, DEA, Boundary Commission, Public Health, the Reclamation Bureau, and numerous city, state and county bureaus just add to the confusion.

For that reason it is hardly surprising crime has long since become one of the leading growth 'industries' along the border. South of San Diego, in California, the borderlands have turned into a virtual killing ground where illegal immigrants prey on each other.

In El Paso, facing Ciudad Juarez, violence was flourishing even back in the mid-1970s when the teenage Angel started getting itchy feet. And that violence was without doubt connected to the ever-increasing flow of aliens and the constantly deteriorating Mexican economy. And all illegal entrants were breaking the law in order to enter the US so they rarely complained unless seriously injured or apprehended. Hundreds of thousands of people every year fell between the cracks in the system, because the massive forces that were supposed to be protecting them were only geared for arrest and incarceration.

In Juarez, Angel heard about people called 'mules' who were prepared to ferry illegal workers across the Rio Grande into El Paso. The women mostly worked as maids while the men toiled away as poorly paid labourers in the construction industry or as gardeners.

The 'mules' themselves earned anything from $5 to $20 per trip. They would either carry their 'customer' on their shoulder or ship them across the river in a rubber raft.

Angel's mother Virginia often paid a 'mule' to carry her across the Rio Grande if she was in need of work. But on other occasions when she was completely broke she would strip to her bra and panties and then wade across the Rio Grande. Alongside her, men would often strip naked for the same journey so that they could keep their clothes dry for the other side.

Once across, Virginia told her son, she would pay Mexicans 'guarding' holes in the border fence, or blocking the northern exits of makeshift bridges. Back in the mid-1970s, authorities rarely bothered to intervene because the 'guards' would move back into Mexico at the sign of any US activity. They also knew that none of the Mexicans using their 'services' would ever testify against them.

~

Angel's first trip across the border involved using a human 'mule' just like his mother had told him. Upon reaching the northern side for the first time, Angel was told to keep out of sight until the key moment when the border patrolmen were visiting the bathroom.

That was his sign to make a demented dash for downtown El Paso, just a few blocks away, where he soon got lost in a sea of similar faces.

It was during one of those early visits to El Paso that Angel began experimenting with harder drugs. He also started smuggling cannabis back and forth across the border for some of the criminals he encountered in Ciudad Juarez.

But those early trips into the US only lasted a couple of days each because, as Angel later told relatives, he missed his home country and he wasn't yet fully proficient at speaking English, although he vas learning fast.

Now settled in Ciudad Juarez, Angel became involved in another street gang of petty criminals. The all-boy gang were full of machismo and the nearest they got to allowing girls into their group was when they permitted a couple of pretty 14-year-olds to hang out with them on boozy, drug-filled Saturday nights at local bars and clubs.

All the boys, including Angel, carried six-inch-long switchblades, and the leader even had a pit-bull terrier that he took with them everywhere.

The only time when the gang kept a low profile was when they encountered gangs of older boys in the alleyways and narrow streets of Ciudad Juarez. These older gang members were known as *veteranos* and Angel and his friends knew they'd be in trouble if they dared to challenge them.

~

Back in those days there were three main rail lines that connected Mexico with the US.

In Ciudad Juarez, like Puebla, it was a common sight to see animals and children straying placidly along the railway tracks. Local trains to different cities tended to be extremely slow and crowded. Often passengers clung to the outside of cars.

The Aztec Eagle ran to the frontier from Mexico City all the way through to New York on a journey that took three days and two nights. That train was the only one at the time that was hauled by streamlined diesel engines.

All the trains travelled along the same single track. And Angel knew that those trains provided a free ride anywhere he wanted.

~

During his increasingly regular trips across the border, Angel continued to try speaking English, unlike many of his compatriots. He believed that it would help him to survive for longer periods in the US.

He had also heard so much about the easygoing American women and how they loved to sleep with teenage boys. However, his growing curiosity with the US was tainted by the aggressive attitude of some of the people he came across during his early travels. It sent out confusing messages to Angel because he couldn't understand why so many people were dismissive towards him and other Mexicans.

Back in Ciudad Juarez, Angel worked as a car mechanic for one of the city's most successful auto thieves. The man taught Angel all the basics and was impressed by the way the youngster seemed to learn things quickly and efficiently. He had plans for Angel.

Soon the teenager was slipping over the border into El Paso and breaking into cars to drive them away in a matter of seconds. Angel was then paid to deliver the stolen autos to a middleman before crossing back into Mexico.

Many of Mexico's most infamous gangsters had started their criminal careers in exactly the same way.

When legendary cocaine baron Hector 'El Guero' Palma was finally apprehended in 1993 after his private jet crashed near the airport of the Mexican city of Tepic, it emerged that he started his career as a car thief on the streets of Ciudad Juarez at the same time as Angel. By the time the Mexican authorities finally brought Palma to justice, he had hundreds of police officers in his pocket and even dressed in police uniform whenever he wanted to travel. To many in Ciudad Juarez, he was a hero who made millions out of the *gringos*' craving for narcotics.

Angel first began dabbling in drugs himself at a time when attitudes towards narcotics in Mexico were far more relaxed than they are today. Cannabis was openly smoked in the street and the cocaine and heroin trade flourished.

Mexico had always been on the front line – literally. Whenever US politicians complain that Mexico doesn't do enough to stem the flow of drugs northbound, Mexicans always respond the same way: 'Without your demand, there wouldn't be a supply.'

The reality was that hundreds of thousands of Mexicans relied on the drug trade for a living. Although penalties for possession are these days often harsher than in the US, back in the mid-1970s judges and police took a much softer line.

American counsellors at every major Mexican town dealt with hundreds of US tourists each year arrested for using drugs and failing to pay bribes to local law-enforcement officials. The *mordida* – corruption – was part of everyday life in many levels of Mexican society, and paying a bribe was often known as a 'golden handshake'.

That was the way of the world in which Angel Resendez operated.

6

Virtually every establishment along the Avenida de Juarez in downtown Ciudad Juarez that wasn't selling hooch or pulling teeth was a seedy club or bar.

Despite his short height, Angel had little or no trouble getting into the sleaziest hostelries, many of which were run by small-time hoods who'd used his services as a pickpocket or burglar in the recent past.

Some nights Angel and his friends would stroll along the crowded, more respectable strip, or wander into what was known as the ProNaf area. Their aim was to catch some innocent *gringos* out for a night on the town loaded with cash and credit cards.

On other occasions, Angel headed for the torro and matador battles in traditional bullfights at the crumbling Plaza Monumental de Toros. There was also dog racing at the Juarez Racetrack.

But, as his social life began to expand into the

downtown areas of Juarez, he found himself being offered larger amounts of cash to make more regular trips across the border.

Though still in his teens, Angel already had a reputation as a man to be trusted.

~

During those early trips across the border, Angel stuck to the areas near the US because they seemed more familiar. He also continued to only stay a maximum of two or three nights on most trips, especially when he had to steal a car.

But sometimes he would hop a freight train for half a day. Travelling by train was not only free but it inevitably deposited him in a town or community where there might be genuine, law-abiding work.

At 15, he was physically still a child but streetwise enough to survive on his own, thanks to his own inbuilt steely sense of determination.

Angel preferred keeping on the move. He had no wish to make close friends with anyone. During his short life he had already experienced many disappointments with friends and family.

And Angel's near-obsession with learning good English brought some real changes to his life. He started meeting girls in the US towns he descended on and, he told his friends on trips back to Mexico, they were just as easy to sleep with as everyone had said.

Back in Ciudad Juarez, Angel's adventures across the border helped turn him into someone who was given respect by his contemporaries. For the first time in his life, he was somebody.

Angel hung out with older children from the *barrio* neighbourhood. He even joined another more sophisticated street gang called Los Santanicos, who gathered in a crumbling wooden clubhouse close to where Angel's mother still lived.

Inside the clubhouse, scruffy children would be competing noisily for football and pool tables. Many of the youngsters, including Angel, liked a lot of the headbanging rock 'n' roll music that was popular in the mid-1970s.

Angel and his friends would often sniff glue and inhale paint thinner to get high before going out to try to pick up girls. That's when his face grew blotchy and sweaty, but at least it was an escape from the harsh reality of his life in the slums.

During this period, Angel lived with a group of homeless teenagers on the edge of Ciudad Juarez who were known to the locals as *paracaidistas*, or 'parachutists', a clever Mexican nickname for squatters who descend on a piece of land from out of nowhere.

The strip of land where Angel stayed lay between two hills across from an old dump, and it was rumoured to be under the control of a gangster who involved the entire *barrio* in car thievery, both in Mexico and across the border.

As Angel continued leading his bizarre split life between the wasteland of Ciudad and the freight-train lines of the US, he began to find himself caught in a classic predicament. He felt, like many who travelled back and forth across the border, caught between two nations and two cultures. Angel had taught himself English and had a basic understanding of reading and writing that helped get him through most situations. But he'd already started to separate the two lives more and more. He'd seen enough of the 'other' darker side of the US along those railway tracks to know that if he had any children he did not want them raised in the US.

On the other hand, he knew only too well that the one place where he stood a chance of making good money was that same country.

~

The area around Ciudad Juarez and El Paso has always been renowned for its scant rainfall and abundant sunshine. On clear days, Angel noticed he could see snowcapped peaks 150 miles to the south, but it was that border to the north which constantly captured his attention.

A border separates one nation from another. Its essential functions are to keep people in their own space and to prevent, control and regulate movements between those two countries.

A borderland is a region that lies adjacent to a border. Some are physically small because foreign influences are slight. Others are large because such influences penetrate far beyond the border zone.

And the borderland between the US and Mexico is probably the biggest and busiest example of such a zone anywhere on the globe. For, as bad as some things seem to be, the area that runs along this entire border is rich in history, an area filled with legends that go back many hundreds of years. The Rio Grande, polluted and diverted as it is, remains one of the most influential rivers of the world.

The land still in a sense belonged to the cowboys and the *vaqueros*, the hard-nosed miners who'd dug deep into Mexico's resources in order to aid its survival. But, with most of the mines now shut down, scraggy ghost towns were all that was left of these two old cultures. That border was the only thing that tempted Mexicans in search of work.

Tall palms still wave over the coastal prairie, a sub-topical stretch of land still known as the Lower Rio Grande Valley. It remains a citrus and winter vegetable source for much of the country.

Each autumn, thousands of people known as 'snowbirds' arrive from the US trying to avoid the snow and ice of mid-America.

Angel and his gang of thieves used to regularly sneak into the makeshift trailer parks filled with these awkward travellers and steal everything they could lay their hands on.

~

In August 1976, Angel headed off for the border once again, determined to get some work in the orange groves of central California.

After hopping a 'mule' for the princely sum of $5, he

wandered into the centre of El Paso and jumped a freight train that would take him deep into the promised land.

A few hours later, the two-mile-long train ground to a noisy halt in the middle of Brownsville, Texas, having followed a route alongside the border. Angel presumed the train had stopped for traffic and took little notice of the voices he could hear just outside the car.

Just then the huge wooden doors next to him flew open and 12 Immigration and Naturalization Service (INS) Border Patrol officers glanced down at the teenager.

'What's your name, boy?' asked one of them.

Angel hesitated for a couple of moments. He'd been waiting for this day to come and he'd carefully formulated a plan. 'Ramirez,' he answered. 'Rafael Resendez-Ramirez.'

'Well, son. You're about to take the long ride home.'

Angel's first ever-encounter was duly recorded by the border patrol in their incident report book like this: *Arrest teenager illegally hopping freight train in the US. Return him to Mexico through Brownsville.*

By all accounts, Angel was completely unconcerned by his arrest. He hadn't been incarcerated, He hadn't been fined. He'd just been politely escorted back across the border. Both he and his captors knew full well that they had done precious little to deter him from coming back whenever he felt like it.

And furthermore, he'd planted the first of dozens of false names into the US law-enforcement system. The fact it happened to be his uncle's name did not seem to bother Angel.

Back in Mexico, Angel proudly boasted to friends how the *gringo* border patrol had let him off the hook – and then went about planning his next trip to the US.

This time he hopped a freight train heading for the Mid-West and on to the Great Lakes. Angel had heard from relatives and friends that the wages were better further north, and he was desperate for a piece of the action. It was 10 September 1976 – less than a month after his first run-in with border patrol agents.

But no sooner had Angel jumped off a freight train as it shunted slowly through the sleepy railway town of Sterling Heights, Michigan, than he found himself arrested by local police along with three other hobos who'd also decided to take in the local sights.

This time he supplied another false name and, since there was no previous record for that name, he was taken to McAllen, Texas, and returned to Mexico two weeks later.

Being an illegal alien in the US did not seem to carry such a severe penalty after all.

7

Maps featuring the North American railway system resemble the ultimate spaghetti junction. Hundreds of intersected lines curve and charge through the landscape in a manmade maze of steel.

It was the perfect setting for Angel Resendez. One hundred years ago, when most of the lines were first built, entire towns emerged out of prairie land to deal with the influx of people and industry brought by the railway.

During Angel's first few trips on the trains in his mid-teens, he had noticed how many freight trains often chugged slowly through numerous towns and cities. At night, he could see into people's front rooms as they sat down for dinner or watched TV or even had sex. And he became increasingly obsessed with watching, peeping at the events unfolding in those homes dotted close to the rail lines. He also concluded that there had to be many rich pickings for a confident thief.

Soon he got up the courage to hop off the trains, slide into backyards, pick a lock, grab everything he could see worth stealing and then, if he was extremely lucky, make a run for it, sometimes even managing to hop back on the same train before it had shunted out of town. As his confidence grew, he began aiming for the bigger houses near the tracks. In those early days, he concentrated on empty properties.

But eventually he started to take bigger risks. He would burgle one home and then head down the road to one or two others before slipping alongside the tracks to await another freight train.

Over the following three years, Angel became such a regular on the freight trains out of El Paso that he even knew the precise times of their departures and would meticulously plan his route across the border to coincide with the railway timetable.

Back in Ciudad Juarez, he saw less and less of his mother and stepfather. The few days he spent in the city each month would be dominated by drug-taking, boozing and selling off jewellery he'd stolen during his travels across the US.

Angel soon became well known to the money sharks and fences of the shanty towns around the city as someone who would regularly appear with stolen goods.

At the main bus station downtown, Angel kept a locker where he would store money, clothes and the .38 revolver he had acquired after breaking into one house near Detroit.   Angel carried the gun strapped to his leg whenever he slipped across the border. He liked the feeling of security that the gun provided and he knew that one day he'd probably be grateful for having it.

~

In Ciudad Juarez, Angel's success as a thief across the border had been noted by some of the career criminals who wanted to take teenage Angel under their wing. One particularly notorious local crook convinced Angel he should concentrate on stealing cars rather than burgling houses because they were more valuable – and a much more impressive status symbol.

By the spring of 1978, 18-year-old Angel was already an accomplished car mechanic – even though he'd never even passed a driving test, let alone owned his own car. And his skills at stealing a car in literally seconds impressed all his contemporaries.

During that year he headed mainly for Georgia and Florida because the houses near the rail lines in the south tended to be further apart from each other, which made it easier to get away. He'd struck a deal with the car dealers back in Ciudad Juarez that he would drive any stolen auto back across the safest border point, bribing Mexican border-control officers in the process.

As one INS source explained, 'Bringing stolen automobiles into Mexico at that time was a pretty easy deal because US border-patrol agents were only concerned by who was trying to slip into the US.

'We didn't care about the Mexicans going home. To

tell you the truth, the policy was to encourage them all to get through the border as quickly as possible in case they changed their mind.'

Angel and his hot-car dealer friends in Ciudad Juarez knew all this only too well. As a result, the stolen car industry thrived – and Angel was a respected auto thief in a place where such skills were highly regarded.

On rare visits home to his mother's house, Angel would even vividly recount stories of the beautiful *gringo* women he seduced during his travels in the promised land.

Angel seemed to enjoy shocking his mother with stories of his adventures, and Virginia encouraged her son to share his experiences in the hope it would bring them closer together.

~

By the summer of 1979, Angel was spending less and less time in Mexico. He'd moved further east into the centre of Florida where the train lines crisscrossed with great regularity. Angel even found he could hop a freight train in St Petersburg on the Gulf Coast and get across to the Atlantic side in less than a day.

During the early part of that summer, he'd concentrated on raiding the numerous trailer parks that littered the swamplands running through the middle of the state. But Angel had found that many of the people living in their $50-a-week mobile homes were on virtually the same poverty level as his friends and family back in Mexico and the pickings were far from rich. Even the cars tended to be beaten-up trucks that weren't even worth the petrol to drive them back to Mexico. Angel was struggling to maintain his own existence, let alone find enough jewellery and money to start saving for his return home.

One day, he headed down the Atlantic coast on the main railway line that runs south along Interstate 95 from mid-Florida. On the way, he came across more affluent communities like Boca Raton, Fort Lauderdale and, the jewel in the crown, West Palm Beach.

Hopping on and off the slow Florida freight trains, Angel began systematically looting empty homes, finding a lot of valuable goods along the way. He also stole late-model autos and drove them back to Mexico. By the middle of the summer of 1979, he was stealing a car every couple of weeks for his crime bosses back in Ciudad Juarez.

At the city's downtown bus station, Angel rented two more lockers to hold all the cash and some pieces of jewellery that he didn't hand over to the fences immediately. He'd also collected two more guns on his travels.

In Florida, Angel continued his prolific run of good fortune. But he failed to appreciate just how obvious his activities were becoming to law-enforcement officials investigating his numerous crimes along Florida's so-called sunshine coastline.

In late July 1979, Angel travelled even further south to the outskirts of Miami. He broke into a house occupied by a woman who immediately woke up and confronted him. Angel attacked the woman, but she managed to fight him off and he ran out of the house and headed off in her car. She called 911.

Angel was arrested less than two hours later when he tried to drive north through a roadblock 100 miles from Miami. He gave police his name as Rafael Resendez-Ramirez. Officers quickly established the identity of the true owner of the car and matched fingerprints with those at the earlier burglary and assault.

On 6 September 1979, Angel was convicted of vehicle theft, burglary and aggravated assault in Miami and sentenced to 20 years in the Florida State Penitentiary system.

He was 20 years old, looked more like 17, and he'd already noticed how the other inmates in the county jail sneered and blew kisses at him. Angel was in for a rough time and he knew it.

He was about to enter a living hell from which there was no escape.

8

One long-term prisoner in jail for life for a series of vicious slayings once described being incarcerated as: 'If you want to know what prison is like, all I can say is lock yourself up in your bathroom for two months and don't come out. No TV, no radio, no nothing! That will give you an idea of what it's like.'

And life in Florida's State Penitentiary at Starke was as grim as its name suggested.

No one could have prepared Angel for prison. And, even if he had been told what to expect, there is no way he would have believed what he heard.

The first six months after his sentencing were the toughest. If not for the prison medical wing and a constant supply of anti-depressants, he probably wouldn't have made it. On several occasions he seriously considered killing himself.

Of the 3,000-odd inmates at Starke when Angel

went in, he was one of the most vulnerable. He was so terrified by the conditions that he retreated into his own world at first, obeying the rules like a timid, obedient schoolboy.

Angel tried to respect the guards and his fellow prisoners, but of course that was soon interpreted as a sign of weakness and he began to find himself the target of every bully in his wing.

Add to that the fact he got little sleep. The noises inside Starke never stopped; day and night, the prison walls resonated with an incessant cacophony of moans, screams, cries and endless profanities. Often, hundreds of men would scream at the same time.

The food at Starke was barely edible and, during his first year of incarceration, Angel dropped 20 pounds from his already skinny 150 pounds. Everything seemed to be cooked until it was tasteless and most meals consisted of cooked greens, grits, corn bread and something resembling chicken gumbo over flat noodles. Angel was convinced it was not really chicken at all.

Soon the tension rose to nerve-racking levels for young Angel. In the first few months in Starke, Angel later told relatives back in Mexico, he'd witnessed at least a dozen stabbings. One day, a guard was stabbed by a homemade shank and pushed off the second landing of the prison block to his death.

Beatings were a regular occurrence, and there were countless occasions when guards would storm into prisoners' cells and kick them senseless.

But it was the sexual harassment that really took its

toll on the young 'pretty' Angel – and it wasn't just the inmates who took their turns molesting the young Mexican. One of the guards on his landing was renowned for performing fellatio on prisoners at Starke, who in return would get special treatment. The problem was that small, slightly built Angel was getting it from both sides constantly, so any chance of so-called 'special treatment' was highly unlikely.

There were times when Angel wondered who was crazier, the prisoners or their captors. But from his point of view it was really irrelevant. He just wanted to get away from that hellhole as quickly as possible.

The high incidence of homosexuality inside men's prisons throughout the US has been well documented. It is estimated that at least 50 per cent of all inmates are either homosexual or had homosexual experiences while incarcerated. The reason has never been that surprising because the inmate power structure has always been based on exploitation, and the best method to exploit any inmate is through sex.

Angel had quickly discovered that every privilege at Starke, including the right to continue living, had a price on it. Angel had little money, so he was forced to bargain with his body. It was the ultimate piece of human degradation.

With no clearly defined minimum age for commitment to the state penitentiary system, Angel and a group of young inmates found themselves ripe to become 'punks' – young objects of sexual desire. There was no way to segregate the younger inmates from the predatory older males, so Angel discovered there was no place in the prison where an inmate was safe from homosexual advances.

Guards would regularly ignore men having sex together in cells or in the workplace simply because they did not want to ignite the fire of violence that lingered constantly just beneath the surface of prison life. As Angel discovered, his attractiveness to other inmates was just about the only currency he had.

He later claimed he'd shared a cell with three inmates at one stage in Starke and been forcibly raped by all three following a terrible assault. Angel was convinced that the guards deliberately put him in the cell with those men because he was considered 'pretty, new, young meat'.

Angel later told his shocked mother Virginia that he had nearly been beaten to death before submitting. But following the attack it seems that he accepted his fate – although he told one of the few friends he made in prison that he would never forgive the system or the inmates for what happened to him.

Angel polished up on his broken English in order to survive within the confines of Starke. He needed some allies or else he knew that his days were numbered. The only inmates who were reasonable towards him at first were the retarded or insane, but at least they offered him some protection.

A lot of his fellow Latino inmates turned their backs on Angel because they believed he was encouraging the sexual attacks. Eventually, Angel became friendly with some of the most unlikely characters – members of the biker gangs and some of the notorious Aryan Brotherhood, white supremacist fanatics who were not impartial to having a pretty young Latino boy as their 'slave'. At least they could offer him protection, which is more than any of his fellow Mexicans were prepared to do.

Gang membership inside jail, as Angel quickly discovered, was supposed to be reserved for the hard cases and the criminal 'names'.

It was ironic that Angel acted as a 'runner' for members of the Aryan Brotherhood as they had been originally formed to protect white inmates from being victimised by black and Hispanic prison gangs.

At the time of Angel's incarceration in Florida, black gangs were probably the strongest in terms of influence inside prison because they tended to be one unit in each penitentiary. Meanwhile, Chicanos were divided into various gangs where membership was dependent upon what area you came from. Not surprisingly, small, shy Angel was not readily recruited.

Angel's bizarre involvement in the Aryan Brotherhood seems to have come about because he was the object of great affection from one of the clan's most powerful members.

Angel kept a low profile so he didn't upset them – and they were mightily amused to have a Latino working for them. He even ignored the hurtful name that a lot of the Brotherhood started calling him 'Angeline – our little bitch boy'.

It made him sick to his stomach every time they

called him that, but he knew he had to hold his tongue if he were going to survive.

After six miserable months, Angel had discovered that prison life could be made bearable if he started taking an interest in the outside world. And that meant throwing himself into studying.

He was interested in politics, especially the right wing; even the extreme fascist ideals of Hitler and others intrigued Angel. He watched black and Hispanic inmates proving over and over again that they had no shame, or so he believed. He also got interested in the US Libertarian Party and wrote off for membership. The letters he wrote at the time revealed he had a very active political brain despite his lack of education.

Learning about subjects like fascism was a cathartic exercise for Angel. And he continued fine-tuning his English in the hope it world spell the beginning of a new, much more lucrative life once he was released.

Gradually, Angel underwent other changes as well while he was inside Starke. He stopped feeling sorry for himself and began taking his daily two-hour recreation break in the prison yard.

Finding the will to survive in such a brutal environment was important to the development of Angel's character. But behind the pleasant face and quiet demeanour he was noting all the inmates and guards who had caused him distress. He would get his own back one day.

~

One of the most stressful events for inmates during Angel's incarceration in the Florida State Penitentiary at Starke was execution time.

He later told relatives that it was as if the Grim Reaper was hovering over the prison. The entire prison would be locked down. Every inmate confined to his cell while the public gathered just beyond the barbed-wire fences, lighting candles in a bid to draw sympathy for a killer about to die.

All the lights of the prison would then snap off, as the power and light company diverted all the power to the execution chamber where the death-row inmate would be strapped into the electric chair.

For the following 20 minutes or so, every prisoner would count down until the big moment. Angel told relatives that his own heart would start pounding very loudly in the cold wall of silence that had enveloped the entire prison.

Then he felt a sickness in the pit of his stomach. He said it was almost like sitting in the electric chair himself. Then the lights came on momentarily before they were all once again plunged into darkness as the prison generator fed 300 amps and 2,000 volts through the body of its next victim.

An eye for an eye. A tooth for a tooth. Angel shuddered as he pictured the scene just a few yards from his own cell.

~

While in prison in Florida, Angel had read with interest

about another Latino who had been grabbing many newspaper headlines.

Richard Ramirez – the so-called Night Stalker – had terrorised Los Angeles during the spring and summer of 1985. Following at least 13 vicious rapes and murders, Ramirez had single-handedly skyrocketed the sale of deadbolts, handguns, alarm systems, garage door openers, and just about every other home security device in Southern California.

By bringing murder into the homes of middle-class Americans, Ramirez had managed to combine homicide, burglary and sexual deviancy in one break-in to a respectable home. His victims were complete strangers.

The amount of citizens across Southern California he filled with terror far exceeded the number of his actual victims.

Angel was intrigued by the Ramirez case as it unfolded in newspapers and on dramatic TV news bulletins. Not only had he already started using the name 'Ramirez' as one of his many pseudonyms, but he also shared a number of disturbing other personal background details with the Night Stalker. Both of them had no high school diploma. Both had never even had a proper job. Both didn't expend a great deal of effort on personal hygiene. And both were partial to large quantities of drugs whenever they felt like it.

But what caught Angel's attention the most was that Ramirez liked to daub bizarre Satanist pentagrams and other signs on the walls of his murder scenes: Experts immediately questioned the genuineness of the Night

Stalker's devotion to Satan, but it had the desired effect of scaring the general population even more. Ramirez specialised in using pentangles, pentagrams, witches circles and other symbols of evil, sometimes rendered in lipstick, other times in the victim's blood.

He also raped with abandon, shot, sodomised, slashed throats, mutilated, bludgeoned and blew out brains. Men, old women, young women, children. He had no particular favourites.

Angel was fascinated.

~

Discovering the will to live and learn about the world while he was in prison did not blunt the shock of the day Angel would re-enter society as a free man. When that day finally came on 3 September 1985, Angel discovered freedom brought with it many problems that he had never before imagined.

In order to survive the caged heat inside the Florida Penitentiary system, Angel had learned to keep a low profile and not upset people, however much he might have hated them. His slight frame and that deer-caught-in-the-headlights expression on his face hid a thousand fears and trepidations. The smile that used to come to his face so readily when he was hopping trains with hobos back in his teens didn't come so easily now.

Many of the prison staff he came across looked on Angel as a classic weak member of the jail population. But underneath that skinny frame and downward gaze lurked a man who had been emotionally torn limb from limb by his experiences inside jail.

Angel had presumed that, once he got out of prison, he would pick up where he'd left off and return to his life stealing cars, breaking into homes and crisscrossing the US–Mexico border.

But it didn't quite turn out that way. He couldn't sleep. He suffered from a never-ending stream of nightmares and flashbacks about prison life. He got constantly agitated and paranoid. Although physically free, he was psychologically still trapped in that dark and smelly prison cell at Starke.

No doubt psychotherapy would have helped Angel adjust better to life outside. Then he could have slowly put the pieces of his shattered life back together. But no such help was available to a jobless Mexican. The memories of that prison and the beatings and the homosexual rape would linger on in his mind forever.

Angel started to realise that the supposedly big things in life didn't mean much any more. It was the little things – being out on the trains alone with the countryside ahead, the early morning, feeling the fresh air, seeing grass and trees. And he was looking forward to the thrill of driving a car once again.

However, as Angel left prison that September day, he was immediately rearrested by INS officials and deported back to Mexico.

But Angel didn't mind. He got a free ride home and he knew that, thanks to numerous aliases he had invented before his incarceration, he would easily be able to slip back into the US whenever he wanted. He'd already been told by other inmates that fingerprints were not passed on to the INS as long as he could provide a Social Security card and number. He'd worked out a system to beat them all.

Angel's self-education in prison had taught him that he had to be strong to survive. He couldn't undo the past, but he could avenge the pain and suffering he endured. He'd gone into prison a boy and come out a deeply scarred and bitter man.

9

Back in Ciudad Juarez, Angel found that most of his old acquaintances had disappeared. Some of them were dead and others had permanently wandered north of the border to the promised land.

Angel stayed at his mother's place for a few days. He told her horrific stories about his appalling experiences inside prison but got little real sympathy apart from the usual 'It must be God's will' reply.

Angel saw little reason to stay in Ciudad Juarez and decided to cross the border to start yet another new life. This time he hopped a freight train heading right through the middle of the country up towards Oklahoma, a state that he had not spent much time in before. Angel knew he had to avoid all his previous haunts because he might be accused of breaking his parole. But he didn't realise that, in Oklahoma, railway authorities were trying to crack down on the vast number of hobos committing petty crimes along rail lines throughout the state.

In the city of El Reno, the train Angel was travelling on was stopped by railway police and systematically searched for hobos and illegal immigrants, many of whom were heading for the farms further north for work as labourers. Angel and another Mexican tried to make a run for it but were caught less than half a mile from the train.

Angel's plan to avoid detention failed after local police took his fingerprints and established he was the same man who'd just been released from prison in Florida.

Angel, genuinely fearful of another horrendous round of beatings and sexual assaults back in jail, appealed to the authorities not to incarcerate him in the US. He was eventually deported back to Mexico.

'Their attitude was that this guy was a humble, poverty-stricken Latino whose incarceration was serving little purpose, so it seemed to make sense to ship him back to Mexico and save the taxpayer a lot of money,' one INS official later explained.

Angel now realised that, in order to avoid identification problems, he needed to make sure that whenever he was detained during train inspections he should admit being an illegal alien. That way, he believed, there was little chance they would match his fingerprints.

Angel used his experiences to help create for himself a lifestyle that would become a law-enforcement nightmare. He started using dozens of different aliases, looked very nondescript and seemed to float backwards and forwards across the US–Mexico border virtually at his own free will.

As one Texas investigator later explained, 'Criminals like him were impossible to keep track of. If ever he was spotted near the scene of a specific crime, witnesses usually described him as looking normal, like thousands of other illegal Mexicans.

'We had no way of monitoring the movements of a guy like this. And by hopping trains he effectively cancelled out any record of his actual movements across the country. It's no wonder he kept committing crimes. He could just disappear into thin air.'

~

In the six months following his return to Mexico after that run-in with authorities in El Reno, Oklahoma, Angel continued crisscrossing the US, committing petty crimes.

He linked up with another stolen auto dealer in Ciudad Juarez and began stealing cars again, then bringing them south across the border.

But, following one close shave in Texas when he was stopped by the highway patrol and just managed to bluff his way out, Angel stopped stealing autos and concentrated on travelling the rails and burgling people's homes.

In the spring of 1986, Angel and tens of thousands of other Mexicans used to a virtually open border suddenly started to find it much more difficult to get into the US. INS officials and border patrol teams under increasing political pressure to stem the tide of illegal immigrants started a major crackdown. Some of the first places they concentrated on were the Ciudad Juarez–El Paso crossings.

As a result, Angel began using other border points. Then on 1 June 1986, a border patrol in Laredo, Texas, arrested Angel, who was using yet another alias. He claimed to officials that he was a US citizen and proudly showed them his Social Security card as evidence.

The authorities never actually established Angel's real identity on this occasion and he was ordered to appear before a federal judge in nearby San Antonio for sentencing two months later.

When he came up before the federal judge that September, he was sentenced to 18 months for falsely claiming citizenship. Another horror ride through the US penal system awaited.

As Angel later told his shocked mother, 'I knew I'd be treated like shit again.'

He claimed that virtually every morning he either witnessed or was submitted to some kind of sex act involving inmates or staff.

Angel felt like a rag doll being pulled from person to person. He tried to block it all out of his head, but he felt a seething hatred towards the men who abused him.

Even when he'd been assaulted as a teenager by those older boys in the fields, Angel had not felt such shame and degradation as he did during the 18 months he was incarcerated in prison in San Antonio.

Angel became a virtual zombie inside prison, hardly ever talking to any other inmates. Mexican gang members disowned him because he had become in their eyes a '*chica*'.

Angel did a lot of thinking during this spell in prison and he started to develop some even more extreme political ideals. He detested homosexuals – a bitterness made worse by his experiences at the hands of gay and bisexual inmates. He tried to work out where he'd gone wrong and concluded that he needed some normality in his life. Perhaps meeting a woman and marrying her would be the answer. That plan helped him get through prison. He had to look forward to something.

Angel wanted to try and work legitimately once he was released from prison. But he believed the only way he could get ahead financially was by breaking the law.

He had served time in at least three southern states. He'd been on chain gangs, road gangs, in solitary for his own protection... and each had its own distinct flavour.

And the truth of the matter was that anyone in prison would just as soon forget his or her experiences, but they never did. The culture shock of it changes a person forever. In Angel's case it definitely branded him an outcast from the inside. His experiences had started at an early age and steadily got worse.

In October 1987, Angel was released from jail in Texas. His old friends the INS escorted him to nearby Brownsville and watched him walk back across the border, knowing full well he'd soon be back.

~

Back in Ciudad Juarez, life held little appeal for Angel, now 28. Soon he was back on the railway seeking fresh pastures before the cold winter of 1987 kicked in and his legitimate employment opportunities faded out.

Through October and November of that year; Angel worked out a living in Kentucky on tobacco farms. It was hard work but Angel decided to stick at it until the end of the harvest because he was desperate not to be tempted back to Mexico.

By this stage of his life, he was starting to think more like an *Americano* than a *Mexicano*. That bothered Angel because he had formed some strong beliefs and political convictions while in prison for that six-year stretch, including becoming a member of the Libertarians. And life inside prison had further tainted his view of American people.

In an ideal world he wanted to find a nice, pretty Mexican girl, get married, have a couple of kids and then travel across the border whenever his coffers needed replenishing.

He still saw the US as a promised land in some respects. But there was this ongoing belief that the people in the US did not deserve his respect. They treated him badly because he was a Mexican. America was a place to use and abuse.

In December 1987, Angel travelled south by train to Mississippi and Louisiana in the hope he would avoid the cold weather further north. He liked the sleepy southern towns because people didn't bother him in the way they did in other places.

He also found the trains moved much slower in the towns of those southern states. Often they would stop for hours in the middle of relatively affluent cities like Jackson, Mississippi and Shreveport, Louisiana. Those prolonged stays enabled Angel to slip off his train, burgle a nearby home or two, and even manage to catch the same train out of there.

Right through Christmas 1987 and into early January 1988, Angel rode back and forth between Louisiana and Mississippi breaking into houses to steal jewellery and cash.

One time he took a car in Shreveport and headed down to New Orleans to enjoy himself for a few days. That break wouldn't have merited a mention except that Angel ripped off an innkeeper rather than pay a drinks bill he was more than able to afford. When two burly bouncers detained him at the door, he produced a shiny .22 and started waving it around before being wrestled to the ground.

By the time the police arrived on the scene, the weapon was missing, but the cops duly arrested him for possession of a concealed weapon and trying to defraud the innkeeper.

This was a serious situation for Angel. Luckily, the police didn't know that he'd parked his stolen auto on a nearby street. However, his beloved gun was gone so there was no evidence to back up the innkeeper's claims.

Angel gave out one of his aliases and then told police his supposed Social Security number. It all sounded convincing to the patrolmen and, once they had Angel in the back of their black-and-white cruiser, they informed him that on this occasion they would let him off with a warning. The charges were completely dropped.

Angel couldn't believe his luck and hotfooted it out of New Orleans as fast as his stolen wheels could carry him. A couple of hours later, he dumped the vehicle and hopped a train going west towards Texas and the border with Mexico.

He didn't want to push his luck…

10

Life out on the rails hopping trains from city to city and state to state might have given Angel a sense of freedom and an escape from his life back in Mexico, but it could also be very grim at times.

Often he'd jump from a freight car into a world of homeless shelters, cardboard, handout food and seedy characters only interested in his fresh, young Latino looks.

Numerous incidents occurred when he was sleeping in dormitories among dozens of mostly older men. Often he'd struggle to sleep through a cacophony of grunts and groans as some of the inhabitants unashamedly sought out sexual relief.

After injuring his knee jumping from one train in the Midwest, Angel developed a shuffling walk with his head usually pointing down, eyes anxiously trying to avert anyone's gaze. In many ways it summed up his chaotic, unfocused life.

He always put the same foot forward and almost skipped along, very slowly scraping his feet on the sidewalk in the process. He looked as if he'd suffered all his life.

~

Angel tried to avoid sinking into a complete life of crime and degradation by continually applying for legitimate jobs while he was travelling across the US.

He'd often wander into junkyards and such places to ask for work. Other times he'd find a spot downtown in big cities and stand alongside other illegal Mexican immigrants to wait for rich *gringos* to drive up and offer him a day's gardening work or casual labour.

But Angel's hesitant manner didn't always give the right impression to the people out kerb-crawling for cheap labour. He soon tired of spending entire days out waiting to be offered 20 bucks for what often turned out to be a very hard day's work.

However, Angel did once get a semi-regular job that just about summed up the way his life was going at the time. In Los Angeles, he worked for more than a month hauling portable toilets around Southern California on the back of trucks.

The biggest downside to the job was that Angel was responsible for emptying and cleaning the bowls with a suction pipe attached to the truck.

As he later told one relative back in Mexico, 'I'd call it the shittiest job I ever had.'

And when Angel did get his hands on cash, he often

spent it down at the local liquor store or on cocaine from a street-corner dealer.

Angel had never had much of an appetite for food but, when using drugs more and more, his weight dropped alarmingly, according to those he met during his travels.

The other big downside to consuming so much alcohol and drugs was that he got increasingly depressed whenever he didn't have enough money to fuel his habit. That drove him to commit more and more burglaries.

It is clear from the testimony of others that Angel was more involved with alcohol from an early age because drugs were not so readily available to him until he started going across the border regularly.

Many people still regard alcoholism as a weakness of character; the moralists see it as a vice; the law links it to many crimes; but psychiatrists regard it as a symptom of underlying personality problems – and there was absolutely no doubt that Angel suffered badly in that department.

In a sense, he was drinking for relief from his bizarre life. By all accounts, Angel was not an out-of-control drinker but someone who mellowed out when he was under the influence, mainly because it really did help him forget his problems.

However, alcoholism is without doubt a progressive condition. This 'progression' often comes to a head during a social or economic decline and it can lead to what doctors call alcoholic psychoses.

Angel had become a classic example of that syndrome by the time he reached his late twenties. He was often flushed in the face, nauseated, unable to sleep, agitated and shaky. Sometimes he got the shakes so badly when he couldn't afford a drink that his whole body – including his face, tongue and hands – would quiver uncontrollably. He'd become restless, overactive and sweat profusely.

But these shakes were often followed by a much more terrifying syndrome – grotesque, visual hallucinations in which Angel started seeing strange animals, distorted human faces and figures. This delirium would usually subside after a few days or whenever he could manage to get a drink.

Angel also found himself suffering from suicidal thoughts because he felt badly about the way he behaved when he was under the influence of alcohol.

But there was the main path that alcohol was leading him into – further crime. He found himself turning more and more to illegal acts. Often he'd commit petty crimes under the influence, knowing full well that the booze helped weaken any doubts he might have.

There was also a much more basic motive behind his activities – he wanted to find the money for another drink or hit of drugs.

His psychological condition was steadily deteriorating, but there was no one in his life who could help him.

~

Back in Mexico, Angel had a relatively large sum of cash in his lockers at the bus station in downtown

Ciudad Juarez. He believed that money could help him establish a life away from his criminal activities. A few recent close escapes had made Angel aware he had to take action to avoid any future problems.

Stage one of this plan was to find a new home well away from the slums and awkward family ties of Ciudad Juarez.

Angel took advice from friends and headed 300 miles southeast to an isolated little town called Rodeo. It could only be reached by a switchback road that twisted and turned through the high scrub mountains of Durango and was renowned as a notorious blackmarket centre for cannabis and hot cars.

But Rodeo wasn't the type of place where a stranger just turned up with his bags and set up home. Most unknown faces were given a wide berth by the locals, who wouldn't even talk to people they didn't recognise.

It was a town where local Mafia-style family vendettas were commonplace – and retribution was swift. After the Medina and Renteria families fell out over a drugs deal just after Angel moved to Rodeo, 30 people connected to the two families were shot dead in a matter of months.

Rodeo was the sort of place outsiders avoided. It was perfect for Angel – a man with a past, and a present that he did not wish to advertise to the world.

Angel even bumped into a petty thief he knew from Juarez during his first visit to Rodeo. It helped him make up his mind to buy a home in the mountains.

Property in Rodeo didn't cost much. Eventually after

some haggling, Angel bought his first home for just $1,000 from a local farmer. It was a modest yet clean, white-painted two-bedroom single-storey building. Hardly a palace by anyone's standards, but it must have seemed like one compared to the places Angel had been living in for the past 30 years.

Word soon went round Rodeo that a wealthy young man from Ciudad Juarez had taken up residence in the town. And most important, gossiped the housewives of Rodeo, he was a bachelor. An unmarried man. In small rural Mexican towns like Rodeo, single men were like gold dust.

Soon a procession of pretty young local girls were wandering past Angel's house trying to catch his eye. Angel knew what was going on and was deeply flattered by the attention after years of rejection by most Mexican girls and a few sleazy encounters with supposedly 'sex-mad' American *chicas*.

Some of the women Angel dated in Rodeo at the time recalled him as a quiet, polite man without any ulterior motives.

One girl – now married and still living in Rodeo – said, 'Angel was a sweet man. He was considerate but said little, which did make our time together a little boring. But he was such a good person.'

Angel was soon known as a kind, generous, shy gentleman who never forgot his place in life.

'He'd hold the door open for me and he would always walk behind me whenever we went into a restaurant,' added the ex-girlfriend.

And Angel always paid for everything, which, in a poor community like Rodeo, was an important factor. The average monthly salary in the town at that time was about $20.

In Rodeo, Angel soon became known as a person with connections to some of the most successful hot auto dealers in the nearby cities. But he never tried to use his influence to upset anyone. He'd often sit alone sipping an ice cold *cerveza* in the local bars. Other times he'd get out a guitar and strum a few tunes. And the number of women he dated could be counted on one hand.

Many of his neighbours knew that – like many other men in the town – Angel spent long periods across the border where decent wages were always available.

As resident Pedro Filiano later explained, 'Most of the men in the town were gone for long periods because they had to go to where the work was. It was as simple as that.'

At certain times of the year the town was so empty of men aged between 20 and 60 that one local joked about setting up a male brothel to keep the women happy

The two main 'businesses' that kept men employed in Rodeo were the stolen-car racket and cannabis dealing. But both relied on US supply and demand. The police in Rodeo tended to leave the criminals alone on the basis it was bad for Rodeo's economy.

They brought trade to the stores and bars, so no one wanted them forced out of Rodeo. In some ways they were the town's lifeblood.

Angel's wire-rimmed glasses and shy, almost nervous demeanour made him look anything but a career criminal who rode the rail lines of North America, breaking and entering cars and homes on a regular basis.

And many in the town were impressed by Angel's excellent English. He told neighbours he learned the language at college in Texas – and no one doubted his word.

'He had the kind of innocent, honest face of someone who had never committed a crime in his life,' said one neighbour. 'You couldn't help trusting him.'

Just a few streets away from Angel's modest home was the Fray Bartholme de Casas convent school, which was opposite Rodeo's only police station. It was run by nuns whom Angel frequently met when he was out on the streets of Rodeo.

The nuns were so impressed by Angel's knowledge of English that one summer they asked him if he would like to work at the convent teaching both the nuns and some local children English.

Angel jumped at the chance. It was an opportunity to walk away from the life of crime he'd been leading since the age of six. The wages on offer were low but with his cash from recent burglaries and car deals Angel decided to give it a try.

Angel turned out to be a very good teacher. Those at the convent recall him being patient and understanding with the children. He had a way of putting things into words that ensured everyone knew what he was talking about.

Both family and friends have since speculated on the reasons why Angel turned his back on a life of crime to teach English to nuns and orphans. There is a genuine belief that he wanted to lead a 'normal life'; that he was trying to get away from criminal temptations. Psychologists naturally presume Angel was trying to start a new life because he regretted his past actions.

Whatever the truth, it is a matter of record that Angel took that low-paying job as an English teacher at the convent, and as far as anyone can remember he didn't miss one day's work.

He is fondly remembered to this day as someone who not only spoke exceptional English but was also good at spelling and grammar.

What baffles Angel's family and friends is how he managed to learn all that despite not attending school after the age of six.

Angel Resendez was already proving he was capable of *anything*.

11

In the late summer of 1988, Angel suddenly quit his job at the convent. No one in Rodeo knew why. But money seems the most likely reason.

So, after many months of stability, Angel headed off to one of his favourite border-crossing points near El Paso. From there he hopped a freight train heading up towards the Midwest where he planned to rob a few houses and maybe even work in the fields.

Angel ended up in St Louis, Missouri, after failing to find any work in the fields. Desperate for money and convinced that the more identities he had the more likely he would be to avoid any problems with the police, Angel tried to obtain a new Social Security number under yet another false name.

But a sharp-eyed clerk at the Social Security office in St Louis immediately cross-referenced the name he gave with Angel's personal characteristics. He was immediately arrested, and police found a .22 in a gym bag he was carrying. He was then thrown into the county jail.

Before Angel's appearance in court in St Louis on fraud and weapons possession charges, prosecutors conducted an exhaustive search detailing Angel's chameleon-like behaviour, which seemed to often have no particular purpose.

As one investigator later recalled, 'It was almost as if he simply enjoyed playing the games even if they were not for any particular reason.'

During his trial in St Louis, prosecutors told the jury that, no matter how many different names Angel might go under, he was the man behind the crimes.

'All the evidence shows that this defendant and no one else is the guy who's bouncing around the country representing himself as Daniel Edward Arnold or Daniel Eduardo or some variation on that name,' Assistant US Attorney Michael Fagan told the jury.

In mid-November 1988, under the name Resendez-Ramirez, he was convicted of 16 federal counts involving using aliases to obtain false Social Security numbers, submitting false statements to the Social Security Administration, unlawfully possessing a firearm and being in the United States illegally and without permission. The judge sentenced him to 30 months in prison.

This time, he was warned by the judge, he would have to expect to serve the full sentence. He was also told that when it was time to leave prison in Missouri he would be transferred to Miami to serve another sentence for violating the conditions of his parole for that 20-year sentence he'd earlier received.

~

Angel obviously didn't want to return to prison following his nightmare experiences on previous occasions.

He knew he'd end up being abused the moment he was incarcerated. He was also growing increasingly confused about his own sexuality. He felt attracted to women, but the need for sexual release made life in prison even more difficult to handle.

Angel had undoubtedly changed since his last prison sentence. He was more aware of the dark forces that lurked at the fringes of his consciousness, born out of sheer frustration and nurtured by the anger of bitterness he felt about his situation in life.

At times, he grew extremely bitter and self-destructive and became almost uncontrollable. Angel tried to release all this rage a little at a time, but often its power frightened even him. He did not like not being in complete control.

But in prison this inner rage served some useful purpose because it inspired him to have the courage to survive without always being the victim of some stronger, more evil inmate or guard. Angel eventually became known as someone whose sheer unpredictability meant he was afforded at least some respect.

And that was how Angel got through his sentence in Missouri. Once again he spent hours every day in the library poring over reference books, historical biographies and newspapers. He even joined an anti-abortion and anti-homosexual group to whom he sent letters on a regular basis. He was clearly very angry about certain issues.

To Angel Resendez, the inmates and guards represented the United States of America – and they were for the most part a pretty bad bunch of people. As he read more and more, he began to dislike Americans even further. He convinced himself they locked him up because he was Mexican and he wanted to prove he was their equal.

Angel's inner anger was such a common ailment among inmates in the penal system that not much notice was taken of him. The only time he did anything to counter the psychotic fury that was steadily building within him was when he and other prisoners lined up for tranquillisers outside the prison treatment room. Often they'd be unshaven and thoroughly dishevelled after just getting their wake-up call.

Once a week, as soon as his wing was unlocked, Angel and others would appear outside the treatment room where two nurses would walk out with a wooden tray that contained several bottles of tablets that were too dangerous to leave unattended.

Many of the inmates were on regular medication prescribed by the prison doctor. It was not difficult to become a medication junkie inside prison. As far as the staff were concerned, it kept the inmates quiet and made them less troublesome

Over the 30 months he spent in prison; Angel was prescribed Librium, Valium, Triptych, Largactyl and at least half a dozen other drugs. Sometimes he was allowed a cocktail of drugs when it was decided that he had built up a resistance to certain individual medicines.

The medication had a similar effect to alcohol in that it shut down whole levels of thought in Angel's brain.

Those drugs really were his only escape.

~

In January 1991, the INS transferred Angel to its Miami district facility, where he was held for five months before being deported through El Paso in May 1991.

As had happened so many times in the past, Angel was happy to be dropped off at a familiar border-crossing point. He headed straight into Ciudad Juarez, and visited family and friends. He headed down to his lockers at the bus station and took out one of his guns. The need to keep moving and the lure of the railway cut short his stay.

For the following six months, Angel made regular trips across the border and hopped trains heading all over the United States. He didn't bother seeking work in the fields. Instead, he concentrated on burgling properties close to the train tracks.

Often, he'd wait until a train came to a halt on the built-up edge of a town before jumping off, breaking into a house and hopping back on to the same train before it restarted its journey, as he had done before.

Angel's priorities were jewellery and cash. And he

was nearly always armed during his lightning raids. No one to this day knows if any of those properties were occupied at the time. If they were, then it seems highly likely he would have encountered people. There must have been victims along the way.

In the early part of 1992, Angel travelled farther west on the railway and began breaking into homes in some of the more isolated communities of New Mexico.

On 3 March 1992, he entered a single-storey house close to the tracks in Las Cruces. But the owners were there at the time and he was grappled to the ground after trying to punch out a man virtually twice his size. For some reason Angel was not carrying a gun then. Police arrested him and a month later he pleaded guilty to aggravated residential burglary. He was sentenced to 18 months in prison.

This time Angel found himself in the Western New Mexico Corrections Facility in Grants. It seemed like a five-star hotel compared with the other prisons. He kept a low profile and was noted as an exceptionally well-behaved inmate. As a result, he was paroled and released in Santa Fe after serving just one year of his sentence.

It is impossible to keep an exact track of Angel's movements at this time except through his propensity for arrest at the hands of police, immigration or any of the other government agencies.

But, just over a month after his release in Santa Fe, Angel was arrested in Panhandle, Texas, while driving a stolen pickup truck. Inexplicably, he was sentenced to just 29 days in jail for evading arrest.

If his criminal background had been properly checked, he would have faced a much longer incarceration. But Angel had built up a vast collection of aliases, and on this occasion his trickery worked like a dream because it helped him avoid spending the following five or six years in jail.

This lenient treatment allowed him to carry on committing more and more crimes – and taking bigger and bigger risks in the process.

Over a two-year period, he was rarely seen in Rodeo except when he returned for a couple of days loaded with jewellery and cash. Occasionally, he'd be driving an automobile with US plates, which he would then sell to one of the stolen-auto dealers in the town.

On those brief visits to Rodeo, Angel seemed relaxed and happy with his lot. No one questioned the source of his income. There were many others in the town who seemed to be working on similar 'jobs'.

Each time he returned to the US, Angel moved farther and farther west. He liked the heat of California and Arizona, which made him feel more at home.

Angel often came across other illegal immigrants when he hopped a train in the west. But he didn't join forces with many of them because it attracted attention to himself. Random checks by INS and railway officials were a daily problem and he knew he could move faster on his own.

On 19 August 1995, Angel was on the Burlington Northern and Sante Fe Railway going through San

Bernardino, California, when dozens of rail police swooped on freight cars and detained two dozen hobos.

When officers searched Angel's gym bag, they found a loaded .22 handgun, so he was immediately handed over to San Bernardino Police. This time, he claimed his name was Jose Konig Mengele. It was Angel's idea of a little in joke to name himself after the notorious Nazi doctor.

No one can officially confirm precisely what happened next, but it seems that Angel talked his way out of police detention and headed back to Mexico. Once again, lacklustre policing had allowed him to get straight back to what he knew best.

~

Now 33, Angel still had the slender figure of his youth. And his neatly cut brown hair remained thick and strong. But his face was lined and sagging way beyond his years.

There had been a saying when he was in prison: 'It doesn't show on your shoes.' If it had, then Angel's would have been battered and worn out. As it was, his face bore the brunt of the stress and strain of incarceration and his life on the rails.

What in his youth had been pleasant, almost handsome features were now deeply lined. Time behind bars had taken each and every part of that young face and etched age and despair across it.

His once-smooth forehead was deeply rutted with lines that made a perpetual frown. His eyes had sunk deep in a morass of crow's feet until it now seemed as if they peered out from deep pits.

His skin was stretched drum-tight, highlighting bony cheeks and jaw, almost as if the skull beneath were trying to force its way through. Its texture was waxy and lifeless.

But the saddest of all Angel's features was his mouth. The loss of some teeth had caused it to sink in and out around his lips unevenly. He was conscious of this and would try to shield his mouth with his hands when he spoke.

All in all, it was the face of someone who had been under intense pressure. He tried to carry himself proudly in prison but his shuffle didn't help. In shyness, he would often tilt his head to one side. After serving almost a quarter of his life in prison, Angel walked as if he was still locked up – as if his life depended on it.

His experiences had shattered his self-confidence and by the time he got out of jail in New Mexico he didn't really care what route his life took, just as long as he could remain in the free world.

He had plumbed such depths of emotional trauma that only his will to keep on the move would help him survive. He trusted no one but himself and sometimes he even doubted his own sanity.

12

About this time, Angel's former hometown of Ciudad Juarez earned itself the title of unsolved murder capital of North America – because of almost 100 unexplained homicides of young women.

Most of the victims were unskilled factory workers, but the vast number of cases prompted Mexican authorities to call in the FBI and independent criminal profilers in the US for help. There was a real fear that a serial killer was loose on the streets.

But not even those experienced law-enforcement officials could establish who was responsible for the murder epidemic sweeping the city and the countryside areas of Chihuahua.

~

In 1995, during one of his rare trips back to Rodeo, Angel met a pretty young lab analyst called Julieta

Dominguez Reyes when he was out shopping in the town centre. She worked at the town's public health clinic and was proud of the fact she hadn't missed a day's work in the three years since she'd started her job.

Angel was impressed because very few of the women in Rodeo had jobs in the town. Most slipped across the border to earn money by working as maids. Anger also liked Julieta because she had no interest in going to that so-called promised land north of the border.

Julieta liked the way Angel asked her out for a date but made no attempt to even kiss her. She was also impressed by his good manners. Angel put Julieta on a pedestal compared with all the 'easy' American girls he claimed to friends and family that he had slept with.

Like most young women in Rodeo, Julieta wanted to settle down, have a family and live happily ever after. She soon became convinced that gentle, quiet Angel Resendez would make the perfect partner. Angel knew perfectly well what Julieta had in mind. He liked the idea of moving her into his comfortable house because then he'd have someone to come back to after his trips across the border.

The couple eventually became lovers and Julieta happily accepted his invitation to move into his house. Angel told her that he would regularly go north to work in the tobacco fields of Kentucky or the asparagus fields of Washington. He also said he picked oranges in California and harvested rice in Texas.

Angel even told Julieta he sometimes got odd jobs in petrol stations in the US, but said he usually stuck to working the fields. It sounded to Julieta like her hardworking new boyfriend had 'green fingers'.

And Angel made sure Julieta had enough money to look after the house when he went away. He always sent home $140 a month, which was a vast improvement on the $6 a week those nuns were paying him to teach English at the convent.

But Angel didn't tell Julieta that he'd also started earning extra cash by using his superior knowledge and experience of the border crossings to shepherd illegal aliens into Texas at a vastly inflated rate of $400. This wasn't a quick hit like the 'mules' because Angel would ensure that the illegal immigrant was taken all the way through until they were safely in the middle of a US border town.

Occasionally, he'd use the cash he'd earned to buy bargain autos he'd drive back across the border and sell for a profit in Mexico. It was a lot less risky than stealing them, but it didn't happen often. Usually Angel wasted a lot of his money on drugs and booze.

Julieta and Angel seemed to have the perfect relationship those first couple of years. She continued working at her job at the public health clinic and he carried on making what seemed to be lucrative trips across the border.

'When Angel came home he was never violent or sadistic. He was a gentleman in all the small details. He never failed to open the car door for me. We were very much in love,' she later recalled.

Angel even made a point of telling Julieta that,

although he sometimes hopped on freight trains to save money, he was not particularly keen on riding them. Angel had even told Julieta about one conviction back in 1988. She was convinced there were no secrets between them.

Angel also told Julieta about the anti-homosexual, anti-abortion group he had joined when he was in prison in the US. He didn't elaborate much about them, but from the way he raised his voice when discussing such issues it was clear that he felt strongly about them.

But what Angel didn't tell his young lover was that he had created numerous aliases and four different birthdates since first hopping the trains 15 years earlier.

By the early 1990s, authorities in the US were under the impression Angel's real name was Jose Angel Rayes. But they also knew him by the following names:

Jose Reyes-Resendez
Jose Angel Reyes Resendez
Jose Angel Rasendez Rayes
Jose R. Angel
Jose Konig Mengele
Antonio Martinez
Antonio E. Martinez
Carlos Rodriguez
Pedro Jaramillo
Lionzo Anger Reyes-Resendiz
Daniel Arnold
Daniel Edward Arnold
Carlos Cluthier Eduardo III
Daniel Eduardo III

Jose Jaramillio
Pedro Argel Resemez Ramirez

His dates of birth were as follows:
Real DOB: 1 August 1959
1 August 1960
15 August 1960
18 August 1960

Other ways to positively identify him were through the
following:
Master FBI 109457R8
FBI number from California arrest 971537AB0
California SID CA11239099
Texas SID TX05118223
Florida SID FL01452046

Sometimes it even seemed that Angel himself was
confused about his real identity. On one occasion in St
Louis, he registered in a city homeless shelter, giving his
name as Angel Reyes, but later said his real name was
Daniel Eduardo III. Then he showed two different
Social Security cards, both of which were false.

But the key to Angel's ability to set up so many
different identities was that he simply didn't stand out
in a crowd. Sometimes he'd wear glasses, other times a
moustache, other times he'd be clean shaven.

Back in the early 1980s he had kept his hair short
and wore serious-looking thick, black horn-rimmed
glasses. Then he let his hair grow so he looked more

like a student. A goatee beard soon followed. Later, he grew that into a full beard before switching back to a moustache and metal-rimmed glasses.

He even tried to hide some of the scars he'd picked up from injuries caused by jumping trains at high speed. These included marks on his right finger, left arm, left forearm, left wrist and forehead.

And sometimes he tried to hide a tattoo of a snake on his left forearm that he'd got during one spell in prison. It was a very positive means of identification.

~

Soon after moving Julieta into his home, Angel returned to work in the tobacco fields of a farm in Russell County, Kentucky. He also sometimes dropped in to see some cousins who lived in nearby Louisville.

Angel became quite a familiar sight in homeless shelters in Louisville. They were free, although not exactly luxurious. Sometimes Angel even made himself a few dollars by giving donations at local blood centres.

Despite all the drugs and sexual activity over the years, Angel still had disease-free blood that was worth selling.

And it helped keep him on the tracks...

Even when Angel was working in Russell County, in the heart of Kentucky, he would sometimes slip off the estate and break into a few nearby houses. But he was careful not to sell any of the jewellery locally. Angel simply kept it all in two sports bags he constantly carried with him.

In the bottom of one of those bags was a .22 handgun. When he was breaking and entering houses, he still kept it strapped to his leg. He also liked to have it for protection when he was hopping trains.

A vast, dangerous world stood between him and economic prosperity.

13

Lexington, Kentucky, became the antebellum '
Gateway to the South' in the 1800s. Its proud
inhabitants carved their city from the rugged Kentucky
wilderness and welded it into a dynamic metropolis of
driving civic pride and fierce hometown loyalty.

Then the railway came and brought great
commercial riches and all the businesses that went with
it. The railway also allegedly carried Angel Resendez
into the heart of Lexington's university district on the
baking-hot night of 29 August 1997.

On that same evening, student Christopher Maier,
22, and his girlfriend had been to a party held by
friends from the University of Kentucky.

They'd decided to head over to another party and
began walking along the side of the main train track
that runs through the university campus on the edge of
Lexington. It was late, but neither of them felt it was

unsafe as they had travelled along the same area many times before.

At one point, the girl thought she heard something rustling in the bushes near by but decided it must have been a stray dog.

Then suddenly a man appeared out of the bushes. He had what appeared to be a knife in his hand and immediately stuck it into Maier's side.

'Gimme your money,' said the man.

'We don't have any,' responded the couple.

The man, whom the girl later identified as Angel Resendez, then got extremely angry.

He ordered the couple to sit down next to the bushes and pulled out some rope he had in his gym bag. They were petrified and did everything he told them to do. They were praying that he would not hurt them. Maier even told Angel, 'I'll go get you some money. You can have my car. Anything. Please just don't hurt my girlfriend.'

But Maier's brave response simply seemed to make Angel even angrier, and they could see the hatred growing in his eyes.

The girl then watched in horror as Angel struck her boyfriend on the head with a blunt object. Then he hit him again and again. She knew she was watching his life slip away in front of her very eyes.

Then Angel moved towards the girl.

She pleaded with him to help Maier. For a moment, Angel stopped in his tracks and went back to examine the student.

He looked down at the young student's lifeless body lying on the dusty ground and told the girl, 'You don't have to worry about him no more.'

Then he moved back to the girl and began furiously punching her in the face. He broke her jaw and eye socket and cut her head and neck with the rings on his knuckles. The attack was so relentless that the girl eventually passed out. He raped her, before dragging her body over to the bushes. He tore down branches with which covered the two bodies. Then he left her for dead by the side of the railway tracks.

Angel Resendez is then alleged to have hopped a train out of Lexington, convinced that by the time police found the two corpses he'd probably be safely back across the Mexican border.

The girl recovered consciousness and fought off the branches that had been so carefully laid over her body. Knowing her assailant had left her for dead made it all the more terrifying because she didn't know if he was still near by.

Next to her lay the corpse of her boyfriend – the first alleged victim of Angel Resendez. She started screaming but blacked out once again when she saw his body.

As she later explained, 'I wanted to crawl in a hole and never come out again, but that would have meant that I let this monster take me away.'

It was still dark when Lexington Police got a call following the discovery of Maier's corpse and his badly battered girlfriend. Paramedics on the scene didn't even realise she was alive when they first stumbled upon her body. They established a pulse and immediately rushed her to the nearest hospital.

Lexington law-enforcement investigators soon flooded the residential street, parking their vans and cruisers in such a way that the vehicle spotlights washed down the area with an eerie white light. One officer retrieved his video camera from his car, hooked up the power pack and joined a still photographer at the scene, while another uniformed officer took measurements with tape. A cloud of steam rose up from the already decomposing body as its gases struck the cooler night-time air.

Two homicide detectives then crouched together and turned the body over on its back while they examined it carefully for signs of cause of death. They didn't need to look any further than the back of Christopher Maier's head for ample evidence.

As one later explained, 'What stunned us was the sheer force and anger with which those wounds had been inflicted. This was not a reluctant killer. This was a guy with the devil in his soul.'

The two stunned detectives walked back to their sedan to wait for the body to be picked up. At seven o'clock, just as dawn came into focus, a coroner's station wagon slid along the quiet street in the direction of the police entourage. Maier's body was carefully bagged and lifted aboard.

The investigators then watched as the wagon left the killing ground for the county morgue.

~

The early days of the Christopher Maier murder investigation yielded no clues that pointed to any prime suspect, let alone a Mexican transient called Angel Resendez.

The victim's girlfriend was in such a traumatised condition that the only description she could provide would have fit just about every Mexican migrant worker in the state.

Investigators were convinced that whoever had done it would have jumped a train shortly after the attack, which meant there was little or no chance of catching them.

Lexington Police had so few clues as to the identity of the killer that they entered details of the murderous attack into the FBI's Violent Criminal Apprehension Program (VICAP). Not one possible suspect's name came up on the computer screen.

It seemed as if whoever had murdered Christopher Maier had got away with it. The file on the killing would obviously remain open but investigators admitted they'd probably never apprehend the killer unless he struck again.

~

Shortly after the murder was committed, Angel enrolled in evening classes back in Rodeo to improve his English. He told his lover Julieta he wanted to spend more time in Mexico. Naturally, she was delighted.

Angel studied English from September 1997 to June

1988. Significantly, there is little record of him travelling across the border during this period.

At college in Rodeo, teachers noticed that, while Angel's English speech was excellent, he needed to further improve his reading and writing, although it was much better than most of the other adult students.

Angel threw himself into the college and impressed everyone with his diligence, and reliability. He was in the words of one teacher 'a good student'.

14.

The first days of November 1997 gave a warning that the chilling discomfort of winter would soon arrive in Lexington, Kentucky. The blustery winds that swept through the city took on a hard bite that sent most folks in search of heavy jackets and wives to the closet for additional quilts for the bed. Outside chores were accomplished with a quicker step, the reward for their hurried completion being a return to the warmth indoors.

Men lingered longer over their hot drinks in coffee shops, and women hurried from their cars into the grocery store or post office, no longer stopping to chat in the parking lot. To the casual observer, it appeared the people of Lexington had fallen back into a normal routine. Below the surface, however, a pervasive feeling of despondency pervaded the area.

Residents were still extremely fearful about the unsolved slaying of Lexington college student

Christopher Maier. At first, people had tried to discourage speculation about the murder. But it soon became clear that discussion of the tragedy was the prime subject on everyone's minds.

There were reports that the killer had been a transient who jumped from a train and then used the exact same mode of transport to disappear into thin air. The real fear among those living near the railway was that he might strike again.

~

Back south of the border in the bars of Rodeo, Mexico, Angel Resendez sipped glasses of iced beer and pontificated about the liberal US and how the women were whores who had abortions and the men were all rabid homosexuals. He assured anyone who would listen that the US would eventually implode, leaving Mexico with an opportunity to become one of the world's leading nations.

It was music to most locals' ears and Angel spoke with such conviction and passion that many of them believed him. He seemed so much more knowledgeable and clever than most of the men who went to the local bars.

Of course, no one realised that some of the items of cheap jewellery Angel sold from his sports bag came from the corpse of a man he had allegedly murdered.

Angel's girlfriend Julieta then delighted her family by announcing she was pregnant. Friends and neighbours in the town later recalled that Angel was ecstatic about the news.

Angel promised Julieta he would continue spending more time in Rodeo rather than across the border. But he did point out that, with a family now on the way, he needed to continue earning decent money to keep them all.

He told Julieta about the other jewellery and watches he'd been keeping in those lockers at the bus station. He said he'd bought it all cheap in the US and assured Julieta it would help keep them all for quite a few months.

She was delighted that they had the money to survive. She was even more pleased when Angel insisted on massaging her legs that night to relieve the stress and strain of her pregnancy.

Julieta was thankful for having such a kind, considerate boyfriend.

~

A few days after Julieta announced her pregnancy – 2 October 1998 – Angel jumped from a train as it travelled slowly through the small Texas town of Hughes Springs, a tiny community with a population of 2,500.

Minutes later, he allegedly broke into an isolated house through an unlocked ground-floor window, crept up the stairs and clubbed 87-year-old Leafie Mason to death before helping himself to cash and jewellery.

When her body was discovered a few days later, investigators found evidence that the killer had sat and 'played with the body' before helping himself to some food from the fridge.

This was the moment, it is alleged, that Angel Resendez became a spree killer.

~

Christmas 1998 was on the horizon. Up north, the *gringos* had just celebrated Thanksgiving, and Rodeo, like so many other Mexican towns and cities, was beginning to copy them; many families with relatives in the US liked to enjoy 'El Tenksgeevee' as they called it. In Spanish, it is *el dia de la gracias*, though Angel always wondered exactly what Mexicans had to give thanks for about a *gringo* celebration. He later said, 'Perhaps we are expected to thank God that the Pilgrims landed in Massachusetts?'

In the *barrios*, orphanages and garbage dumps of cities across Mexico, hope stirred as the cold descended. In spite of everything he had done, Angel knew that his pregnant girlfriend Julieta would be looking forward to a good Christmas. He'd even visited the local convent where he'd once taught English to make a donation towards gifts for the town's slum kids.

Angel promised the nuns he would try to make sure he and his young girlfriend attended the Christmas pageant at the end of the month.

The nuns opened their doors to everyone at that time of year in the hope that somehow the Christmas plays would evangelise all the *barrios*, pulling together the Catholicism that the entire nation shared.

Then Angel informed Julieta he needed to visit the US

for some work that could bring them great riches in the run-up to Christmas. She asked him to hurry back as quickly as possible. He nodded in agreement and headed out of Rodeo with his familiar gym bag in his hand.

On 17 December 1998, Angel Resendez is alleged to have jumped off a freight train in the Houston suburb of West University Place, which has a population of around 13,000. He'd spotted the next house he intended to rob from the train. It was in the 4200 block of Lehigh Street, right alongside the railway tracks.

The house itself was a new three-storey brick structure with a peaked roof. It stood out as something special compared to many of the smaller low-slung wooden bungalows that dominated the street. The owner of that house – Dr Claudia Benson – was known as a 'real nice lady' who frequently walked along Lehigh Street with her daughters as they headed to the video store at the end of the block.

There were no lights on in the house as Angel pushed the top of the garage door and then released a connection to the electric garage door opener. Although Angel didn't know it at the time, there was an alarm system, but it had been switched off.

He then slipped into the house through a door from the garage. Within a couple of minutes, Angel had helped himself to jewellery, a CD player and some cash when he heard that same garage door open and shut.

The owner, Dr Benson, 39, had just arrived home in her Jeep Cherokee. Her husband and twin daughters were out of town at the time. She worked at the

Baylor College of Medicine where she was training in genetics research.

As Dr Benson walked into the house, Angel grabbed her and dragged her up the stairs to the main bedroom where he produced a knife he had stolen from her kitchen and stabbed her three times before clubbing her at least 19 times in a frenzied attack. Then he sexually assaulted her. The bloody knife was later found next to her body.

Then he stumbled into the garage and tried to smash the lock that was attached to the steering wheel of her Jeep. Eventually, he snapped it in half and drove off in the car.

The killing of Dr Benton sparked fears that a madman might be on the loose in the area. Police had few clues to the identity of Dr Benton's cold-blooded killer.

Gary M Bryce, Chief of the West University Place Police Department appealed to reporters within hours of the killing: 'Any kind of help we can get in locating this individual would be greatly appreciated.'

They'd already checked Dr Benton's husband's alibi and knew there was no way he could have been involved in the murder. To further confuse investigators, another murder had been committed just a couple of weeks earlier at a wig shop near the Benton residence. They struggled to establish if there was a connection.

Two days after Dr Benton's body was discovered, her Jeep Cherokee car was found in San Antonio, Texas. The vehicle and her home were carefully dusted for prints but the results of tests would not be known immediately because of the Christmas holiday rush.

It wasn't until the end of December that investigators positively identified Angel's fingerprints left on the broken pieces of her Jeep Cherokee steering lock left outside the house.

They immediately contacted the INS about the doctor's slaying.

On January 7 1999, a Harris County, Texas, magistrate signed a warrant for Angel's arrest in the name of Rafael Resendez-Ramirez, charging him with burgling Benton's house. But they did not have enough direct evidence to charge him with the doctor's murder. Local newspapers appealed to anyone with information about the whereabouts of Resendez-Ramirez to contact West University Police or Crime Stoppers.

If the state of Kentucky – where Angel's alleged first victim had been murdered – had been part of the same forensic cross-referencing crime system, they would have matched up evidence from both crime scenes that would show that the same man was responsible for both homicides.

Angel's other alleged killing of that 87-year-old woman in Hughes Springs, Texas, had still not been positively linked to him.

It was just one of the first of many administrative errors that cost law-enforcement officials their reputations. But, more important, it helped a killer to stay on the streets and railways. A killer capable of inflicting death and destruction on innocent people who got in his way.

~

Over the years he'd lived in Rodeo, Angel had increasingly gained a reputation as a slightly eccentric loner who would go on long bike rides with his mongrel dog Patol.

Local shopkeeper Elvira Marufo recalled, 'He was quiet and polite. He sometimes talked right-wing politics or about Christianity, but the tone of his voice always remained soft and sweet.'

On Angel's visits back to Rodeo in the first few months of 1999, no one noticed any change in his mood since he'd started his alleged killing spree, but then they had no reason to suspect he was like a powder keg just a few emotional heartbeats away from exploding.

Angel would appear back in Rodeo armed with jewellery and cash, which he then sold off to local black-marketeers before announcing to Julieta it was time to head back to the US once again.

As usual, he kept some of the trinkets for Julieta or, as was later claimed, he wanted mementoes of his crimes. And, of course, he was still collecting guns to place in his lockers at the bus station.

Angel's trips across the border helped him lose contact with reality in a profound manner. Thoughts, perceptions, feelings and his behaviour were different when he was not in Rodeo. But his personality was deteriorating at an alarming rate.

He displayed a distorted perception of himself. He'd become deluded and would often imagine he was in the company of someone else when he was entirely alone. These misconceptions compelled him to react to people or situations around him in a bizarre fashion. Angel found it virtually impossible to carry on a rational conversation when he was out of Rodeo. He would spend long periods of time mute and unresponsive even when travelling a train filled with other hobos. He was becoming increasingly detached and out of touch with his own environment.

But Angel's growing psychoses came and went. He could seem perfectly normal one minute and then instantly deteriorate into a psychotic 'episode'. He began to believe that robbing people's homes was actually doing them a favour because they could claim everything and more back on insurance.

However, when he returned to a normal state, Angel would feel ashamed of himself for violating another person's home. But then he'd tell himself that they were American so they probably deserved it.

He'd already proved that he was capable of anything if someone stood in his way.

~

In the spring of 1999, Angel and Julieta's daughter Liria was born. But even before the birth some people in Rodeo noticed that Angel seemed increasingly unsettled.

He even confided in one friend that, despite promising to stay in the town until Julieta had settled at home with their child, he was desperate to return north of the border.

Soon after the birth, Angel took off for the US, having promised Julieta he would not be away for more than a few weeks.

He ended up hopping trains for at least two months. But he did always send back the $140 a month he'd promised to help run the house and pay for their child.

To get that money to Julieta he had to go into telegraph offices and fill in forms before wiring the cash to Mexico. It wasn't a simple procedure and often took Angel an entire morning. But he'd given his word. Julieta and their child represented the safe secure compartment of his life and he did not want to do anything to risk losing that.

In March 1999, Angel was seen at a shelter in Evansville, Illinois, just before he paid yet another visit to his relatives in Kentucky. The murder of student Christopher Maier 18 months earlier did not put him off visiting the state.

In Henderson, Kentucky, near the Illinois–Indiana border, Angel stayed in another local homeless shelter.

A man matching Angel's description and bearing his distinctive tattoo of a coiled snake with 'bleeding' eyes on his left forearm stayed a few nights at the Harbor House Christian Centre and registered under the name 'Jorge Luis Menendez' – not one of his usual aliases.

The shelter director and a resident later saw Angel's picture in a local paper and remembered the tattoo. And one shelter resident recalled rooming with Angel.

In fact, Angel had got some legitimate work at a nearby Tyson chicken plant. He stayed there for three days. Officials at the plant insisted they had no record of a man named Resendez-Ramirez, but they did later admit he might have signed up for temporary work under any number of other names.

15

Many of the residents of Weimar, Texas (pop 2,050), still gathered most weekends for 40-cent lemonades at the Community Pharmacy on Main Street and then pop into Benny's Cafe for their afternoon coffee.

They prided themselves on being completely off the beaten track, although some would disagree, as dozens of freight trains chug through the town every day.

Most of them are pulled by big black-and-yellow Union Pacific engines rumbling through this sleepy hamlet hauling mainly cars, gravel and chemicals.

At 10 pm on 30 April 1999, Weimar resident Reverend Norman 'Skip' Sirnic and his wife Karen made a phone call to the minister's mother and stepfather in Lubbock, Texas, from their isolated home on the edge of town.

The noise of a freight train along the main rail line close by eventually brought the call to a premature end…

Moments later, Angel Resendez slit the screen on the

back door to the Sirnics' home with a knife and attacked them with a sledgehammer taken from their garage.

Some time afterwards, Angel leaned the weapon against the bedroom wall and carted off a videogame system, a VCR, jewellery and other items in the couple's 1998 Mazda pickup.

~

It wasn't until nearly two days later that one of the minister's own parishioners stumbled upon the bodies after going to the house because Reverend Sirnic was running late for the 10 am Sunday service in Weimar.

A few minutes later on that warm Sunday morning, 2 May 1999, Chief of Police Bill Livingstone reluctantly left his place in the pew at church in Weimar to answer his pager. Livingstone knew it wasn't going to be anything he wanted to hear. Generally, he wouldn't get a call on Sunday morning unless it was something bad – and that always seemed to happen when he was off the clock. Thirty minutes later, Livingstone's hunch was confirmed as he glanced down into the familiar faces of two dead people.

The bright sunlight highlighted the awful injuries suffered by the Sirnics and the blue-and-purple blood staining the Reverend's broad, sagging face. The white of his short-sleeved shirt gave way to heavy bloodstains across the chest and stomach. On the left wrist, he still wore a watch. On the left hand, a wedding band to celebrate his marriage to the woman who lay dead near by.

Chief Livingstone carefully stepped to his right to examine the Reverend's wife, Karen, whose crumpled body had been bludgeoned like a rag doll. He knew he shouldn't touch anything until the crime lab boys arrived. Such an examination did not come naturally to Bill Livingstone because he had never had to deal with a homicide in Weimar.

Livingstone stepped back from the bodies with great care. He couldn't quite believe what he'd seen. A senseless, cold-blooded slaying of two innocent people. But why was it committed with such anger and venom?

Livingstone told reporters the perpetrator was 'a sick, sick individual'. No one had been slain in the small community in living memory. 'I had to call in the Fort Bend County Sheriff's Department because we don't even have a crime scene unit,' explained Livingstone.

Within days, the Texas Department of Public Safety advised the Weimar Police to talk to West University Place police officials investigating the death of Dr Claudia Benton the previous December.

The two departments compared and matched forensic evidence taken from both crime scenes and announced that Angel – still known as Rafael Resendez-Ramirez – was their chief suspect in all three killings.

Up in Lexington, Kentucky, authorities still had no idea that Angel could be the same man responsible for the killing of student Christopher Maier in August 1997.

In Weimar, the slain pastor's only sibling, Mark Sirnic, 44, himself a pastor at the Kirk of the Bonnie

Brae in Denver, said he was 'extraordinarily impressed' with the lawmen's efforts.

He'd been told of his brother's death just 15 minutes before he was due to lead worship in his own church. He had no doubts about what his brother and sister-in-law went through. 'They literally didn't know what hit them. There's no indication they were awake... I'm grateful for that. At the same time, the violence is unconscionable, unimaginable.'

Reverend Mark Sirnic remembered his brother, who was also survived by a 19-year-old son from a previous marriage, as a high-energy person who loved to read, garden, exercise with his wife daily and 'play the villain in these silly throw-peanuts-at-the-villain melodramas' the church frequently staged.

Mark Sirnic even conceded that the hunt for his brother's killer had had a confusing effect on him and his family. 'Forgiveness is a slippery concept in some ways,' he said. 'The burden of bearing a grudge is not something I choose to do. But at the same time the reality is that evil has been performed, and the person who did that needs to be removed from society. I have no burning need to see him put to death, but one murder is too many times. Three murders is way too many times.'

~

A couple of days later, news of the Weimar slayings reached Police Chief Randy Kennedy, who'd investigated the killing of Leafie Mason in her home in Hughes Springs, Texas, the previous October.

'I thought it could have been a railway drifter, but we'd run dry on leads here. Then I heard about this guy,' Kennedy later explained.

Kennedy immediately posted details of his unsolved murder in the *Texas Crime Bulletin* and got a call from the Houston Police Department who were investigating some similar crimes.

Within two weeks, he had handed over the palm prints he'd got from the crime scene. The only problem was that there was no record of Angel's palm prints anywhere in the US law-enforcement system.

At 11 am on the morning of 10 May, family, friends and members of the community paid their last respects to the good Reverend Skip and his wife Karen.

As his brother later pointed out, 'Skip was one of the few good people in the world. He was good to the core. I think there are about 2,000 people who live in Weimar, and more than 1,200 came to the funeral; that's the kind of impact he had,' he said.

One of those who attended was retired waitress Josephine Konvicka who had been widowed since 1986. Josephine loved making quilts for her six grandchildren on their birthdays. And at least twice a year her entire family would gather at her home near Weimar for a reunion.

Her son, Houston police officer Thomas Konvicka, a married father of two young girls, visited his mother's house for one of those reunions just after the Sirnic funeral.

At the gathering, the entire family talked at length

about the brutal double homicide in Weimar of the preacher and his wife at their house just three miles from Josephine's.

Josephine Konvicka insisted she felt safe and secure in her neat, detached home where she enjoyed canning vegetables and fruit.

'She enjoyed life like she should have,' recalled son Thomas. 'She was always very cautious, but it was home.'

The family had moved there 30 years earlier. Her children used to ask Josephine to come to Houston to visit them all, but she preferred being at her own house.

No one in that sleepy community believed that the killer of the Sirnics would return.

~

One of the first times Angel Resendez's personal details were revealed in public in connection with a homicide was on 26 May, when the *San Antonio Express-Star* headlined an article: 'SUSPECT IN KILLINGS SEEN IN ALAMO CITY'.

The article claimed that Angel had been seen walking in San Antonio. They mentioned he was linked to three homicides near Houston, prompting authorities to issue a warning to residents living along railway lines. 'Jose Angel-Reyes-Resendez, 38, a drifter who goes by several aliases and guises, is suspected of killing three people, including a preacher and his wife in Weimar, about 90 miles east of Houston,' stated the newspaper.

It was only many weeks later that it became clear that the name issued by police was much closer to Angel's real identity than the details that were later released by the FBI.

~

There is evidence to suggest Angel Resendez apparently had no idea that detectives north of the border had linked his name to the murder of at least three people. Texas law-enforcement officials had posted a copy of the warrant on the worldwide crime website naming Angel. It was supposed to have been read by all agencies across the country.

On 2 June 1999, Angel tried to slip back across the border near El Paso, when he was stopped by an INS border patrol.

The INS later insisted Angel was using several aliases. And the agency's computer system was not linked to any law-enforcement database so they had no way of knowing Angel was a wanted man.

The INS released Angel Resendez and deported him back to Mexico even though West University Place Police in Houston had already issued a warrant for Angel's arrest in connection with the December 1998 killing of Dr Benton.

The Justice Department later claimed the INS *did* have information on their computer about Angel. And when the INS did a file search they must have come up with fingerprints and photos of Angel.

'They had that information. But whether they

handled it appropriately or not is another matter,' said Justice Department spokesman Carole Florman.

It has since become clear that that way the INS handled Angel at that El Paso border point 'raises serious questions about the INS knowledge of the case and procedures used'.

But, even more importantly, that mistake was to have tragic consequences. For alleged serial killer Angel Resendez was free to roam the rails once more.

And it took him just 24 hours to strike again.

16

Teacher Noemi Dominguez was always looking out for her eight siblings. She was a cautious lady with a safe, secure job who liked to tell her younger sister Brenda to keep her doors locked at night and always check out for strange people hanging around near the house.

On the night of Thursday, 3 June 1999, 26-year-old Noemi had decided to stay in at her apartment in Houston and sketch some Japanese animation figures for a children's book she was planning to write.

As Noemi prepared for bed that evening, yet another freight train clattered along the tracks that ran a few hundred yards from her home. It was something she had long since become used to. It is alleged Angel Resendez was on that train.

Minutes later, Noemi Dominguez's crushed corpse lay brutally battered to death in her own home.

Angel Resendez then looked down at the body with an expression of fascination on his face. He studied the blood, the gaping wounds, the omnipresent power – it excited him when he looked at the corpse.

He then spent almost an hour in Noemi Dominguez's apartment, moving to the kitchen where an overwhelming desire to eat took over from his sexual excitement. He opened the fridge and helped himself to some recently cooked chicken and rice and washed it down with a cold bottle of beer.

Once finished, he washed his hands in the bathroom sink and left the apartment as soundlessly as he'd come, taking a few valuables and cash with him. Quickly, but not so fast as to draw attention to himself, he made his way outside to Noemi Dominguez's 1993 Honda Civic. He got into it, fired the engine up and headed off into the night.

A couple of hours later, with dawn slowly creeping across the vast expanse of Texan flatlands, Angel was driving south at high speed. The horizon in the east was deep indigo. It was the time filmmakers call 'the magic hour' when there is no glare in the air and colour and dimension are sharper and more clearly defined.

Angel passed people walking into the fields on their way to the sort of early-morning jobs he knew much about. Overhead a couple of hungry vultures circled the freeway that was dotted with naked brown trees burned by the omnipresent sun.

Eventually, Angel Resendez hit Highway G in Fayette County, just three miles from the tiny Texas community of Weimar where he is alleged to have slain the Reverend 'Skip' Sirnic and his wife just four weeks earlier.

Then he spotted a neat, detached home alongside the highway. It belonged to 73-year-old grandmother Josephine Konvicka who raised cows, lived alone and liked making quilts for her grandchildren.

The man whose double slaying had already shocked the community was about to strike again.

Minutes later Josephine Konvicka lay dead in her bed, having been brutally struck on the head with a pointed garden tool. She was killed in her sleep and it was unlikely she suffered.

Her killer then tampered with the dome light of her car after failing to find the car keys, which were in a drawer.

Angel Resendez stayed in the house and once again enjoyed a meal before departing.

At 7.30 pm on that same day, Josephine Konvicka's daughter Linda Vacek found her body when she and her husband Daniel stopped by to check on her and the cows she kept in a field around the back of the house. 'Linda walked up to the house. I was in the barn... the way she came running through the pasture, I knew something was wrong,' Linda's husband later said.

He remembered his mother-in-law as a loving woman who lived for her family, making those quilts for her grandchildren with her older sister, whom she shuttled to local bingo games. 'She didn't drive – Josie always picked her up.'

Her son, police officer Thomas Konvicka, said that

his tragic connection to the victim made him even closer to the manhunt than he would ever likely be.

'I think to everyone… whether you're in police work or not, it's the same,' he said. 'You see it happen everywhere else, but, when it hits close to home, it's very devastating.'

Soft-spoken Officer Konvicka could hardly bring himself to talk about how his elder sister had found their mother battered to death. 'It's been very hard for her. We still can't quite believe it. As for myself, I'm basically numb.

'My mom loved being where she was. Your home is your security, where you feel safe and where you feel comfortable. For him to violate that is… I don't know how to put that. He had no right to do what he did. All these people would've just given him whatever he wanted.'

Forensic evidence almost immediately placed Angel Resendez inside the house.

Even a hardened cop like Thomas Konvicka struggled to come to terms with the brutal crimes committed by Angel.

'Just the fact of murder never happens much out there, much less a serial killer,' added Konvicka, who left a job in engineering to become a policeman four years earlier. 'It's another thing that is unbelievable.'

Konvicka handled fingerprint identification on a daily basis inside the Houston Police Department. But he was not a direct part of the task force. However, he constantly talked to colleagues about how his mother's case was progressing. He conceded, 'I am too close to this to be privy to any delicate info.'

Konvicka was reluctant to be critical of the INS when he learned they had released Angel on 2 June, days before he was alleged to have killed Konvicka's own mother. 'I'm upset and disturbed. I don't know about angry yet,' he said, pausing to find the right words. 'I need to know the facts. I want to be fair. I'm going to call the INS and see what I can find out.

'It's very difficult to be objective about that, and I'm trying to be,' he added. 'I definitely expect an explanation. It bothers me. We all felt sickened that they didn't make the connection. It shook us all up.'

But Konvicka insisted that he didn't want to specifically point the finger at the INS. 'The main issue is to get him off the streets so he doesn't kill again. Let's stay focused on the fact we need to put him away. We can sort out the rest of the stuff later.'

That included what Officer Konvicka ultimately wanted to see happen to the man who'd bludgeoned his elderly mom to death. He explained, 'I'd like our side to get him. I'd like him to be caught on this side of the border and tried here, in Texas.'

He didn't need to mention that Mexico didn't have the death penalty.

On the same day – 4 June 1999 – the media in Houston, Texas, printed a photo of Angel and linked him publicly with the Konvicka slaying, the killing of the Weimar preacher and his wife, and Dr Benton back in December 1998.

The bludgeoned body of Houston teacher Noemi Dominguez in her apartment had not yet been discovered.

Residents in Weimar and West University Place immediately raised a combined $50,000 reward for information leading to Angel's capture. But investigators presumed the worst – that he had long since slipped back south of the border.

Newspapers described 'Rafael Resendez-Ramirez' as a career criminal and warned that the Mexican citizen had 'tangled with the law since 1976 in Texas, Florida and California'.

West University Police Chief Gary M Bryce – leading the Benton investigation – told reporters in Houston, 'He's been arrested for a little bit of everything but nothing of this severity. He's a very dangerous man. He needs to be caught. He needs to be found.'

Investigators had established matching physical evidence at both crime scenes but Bryce admitted, 'We need to be able to tie the suspect to the victim inside the house to make the murder case. We need comparison evidence.'

The fact that all the named victims lived near railway tracks was also reported in the local press. Even Chief Bryce speculated that the killer 'may have been riding the rails and approached the houses because at the time that may have been what was available'.

But the real significance of this fact had yet to be openly established.

~

On that same Saturday morning – 4 June– Noemi Dominguez's sister, Brenda, had become extremely worried about why her sister was not picking up the phone. She had a bad feeling about it. In fact she'd had that feeling since the first time she'd tried to call her sister late on Thursday night.

They had been due to meet up in Houston, but Noemi never showed – and that was very unusual for her. The two sisters were supposed to be finalising plans to go to a Japanese animation convention in Dallas on that Saturday.

Around 9.45 pm that evening, Brenda and her brother decided to visit Noemi's home and find out if she was OK.

They discovered her clubbed to death in the bedroom of the apartment she rented in a multifamily house in the 6900 block of Van Etten Street, close to the railway tracks. Her 1993 Honda Civic – Texas licence plate JJH 57N – was missing.

Initially investigators failed to establish if Dominguez had been murdered before or after 72-year-old Josephine Konvicka. DNA and blood evidence found at the scene of the older woman's death eventually established she had been killed a few hours *after* Dominguez.

Fayette County Sheriff Rick Vandel summed up the situation when he revealed to reporters, 'Some forensic evidence that has been analysed indicates that the Dominguez lady was killed probably before my lady was.'

Brenda Dominguez was understandably shocked by the brutal death of her sister. 'She was always looking out for me. She was very cautious. She'd get mad at me for not paying better attention to my personal safety. She always looked under her car, locked her doors... She was a really strong believer in God, and I'm trying to be strong for her now.'

On 12 June, police in Del Rio, near San Antonio, Texas, found schoolteacher Noemi's Honda Civic abandoned with a knife placed on the front seat. Officers who discovered the car knew immediately that something was wrong because of the knife.

As one investigator later surmised, 'It was almost as if the suspect was leaving a calling card to warn police that the car was involved.'

The other 'calling card' was even more obvious – the car had been abandoned next to a railway track. It looked as if he was taunting authorities every step of the way.

The discovery of the car also confirmed officers' worst fears – that Angel had escaped across the nearby border with Mexico. As one explained, 'His trail went completely cold. We knew he was on the other side, which made him virtually untouchable.'

It was now clear that Angel was on a killing spree that would not end until he was captured.

Police in San Antonio were put on full alert to be on the lookout for Angel just in case he hadn't left the area. 'All our patrol and traffic officers have been instructed to be on the lookout for this guy,' police spokesman Al Ballew told reporters. 'Everyone's been advised to keep their eyes open.'

But investigators knew he was most probably back in Mexico

17

The news media in Houston named Angel Resendez – or Rafael Resendez-Ramirez, as he was known throughout the nation – a suspect in the Dominguez and Konvicka killings after analysis of fingerprints and her DNA evidence.

As Fayette County Sheriff Rick Vandel said at the time, 'Resendez-Ramirez is a strong suspect. There were similarities enough that were noteworthy... anything's possible right now.'

What authorities didn't reveal was that, after killing both Dr Claudia Benton and Noemi Dominguez, the perpetrator had daubed strange signs in blood on the walls that resembled the patterns left by Night Stalker Richard Ramirez when he struck terror into the inhabitants of Southern California 15 years earlier. Investigators now knew for certain the Mexican they referred to as 'Rafael Resendez-Ramirez' was their man. But they didn't want to scare him off by publicly revealing too much about his methods.

They noted that all of his victims had been bludgeoned during night-time burglaries where the intruder stole, or attempted to steal, their vehicles.

If Angel Resendez's first alleged victim, student Christopher Maier, had had his automobile stolen, then police in Texas and Illinois might have sooner recognised his involvement in the Kentucky slaying.

But for the moment no such connection had been made.

~

It seems that Angel Resendez remained unaware of the manhunt. He slipped back into Mexico after dumping Noemi Dominguez's car near San Antonio.

He then turned up in Rodeo with bags filled with jewellery and watches that he told his common-law wife Julieta to hold on to for him.

During that visit home, Angel was seen by neighbours in Rodeo out riding his bicycle past the local police station and into the countryside beyond. Angel the 'serial killer' was still looked on as a pleasant, simple type of fellow at peace with himself and the world.

On 8 June, Angel further compounded the theory that he had totally compartmentalised his two lives by playing the role of a family man by videotaping a neighbour's child's fourth birthday party.

Lupe Abitia Valdez would often play in the garden of Angel's house because it was much bigger than the one she shared with her father, mother and four brothers and sisters.

Angel was known to many of the local children as 'the teacher' from the days when he taught English at the convent school opposite the police station.

Everyone at the birthday party was impressed by the patience Angel showed towards all the children. The following day he played the video to Lupe and her eight-year-old sister Alexis as all three sat down and munched on corn chips and drank sodas.

But later that same day Angel began to show signs that something was troubling him.

'There is something the matter with me,' he announced to Julieta. The comment came completely out of the blue and she did not know how to respond.

A force within Angel Resendez had become in recent months like a big black hole sucking all the goodness out of him. He'd tried to suppress this force, but now he could feel its presence once more.

The more energy he had put into trying to stay normal, the more it tore him apart. It had been building up throughout his life. It had destroyed his ability to stay at school. It warped his relationship with his mother and many others. And finally, on that dark night of August 1997 in Lexington, Kentucky, it had consumed him as he allegedly committed the first in a series of brutal, senseless killings.

Angel Resendez had been unable to lead a normal life, even though he gave the appearance in Rodeo of being someone who was in complete control of his future.

Before Angel's first alleged kill he'd tried to keep away from houses where people were obviously in residence, so he wouldn't encounter anyone who might trigger his fury.

But by the summer of 1999 it was too late. He was slipping more and more out of control. It escalated to the point where, if he were on a train as it slowed down near any potential houses he'd simply jump off and head for one of them, whatever the danger signs.

Angel had that most convenient of clichés – a split personality – because the 'other' side of him knew precisely what he was doing, and where he was. He also knew that what was inside him was not a figment of his imagination. It was horrifically real.

It meant that, despite professing his undying love for Julieta back in Rodeo, he was probably incapable of truly loving a woman. He couldn't experience love because he'd never grown up with it around him.

There had been times when Angel burst into tears after he'd been nasty to Julieta and begged her forgiveness. But they were tears of someone afraid to be abandoned by that semblance of normality in a bizarre life. They were not truly tears of remorse.

When Angel withdrew into his little shell and took off for long bicycle rides with just his dog for company, he was trying to protect that part of him which he did not want Julieta to know anything about.

That's why he refused to explain his problems to her, even though he'd admitted there was something the matter. He couldn't face the truth within him even though he knew he was very sick.

Some of the most famous serial killers of recent times have 'suffered' in the same way. John Gacy admitted after his arrest that he had to destroy something he felt was active and cancerous inside himself. The ritual of slaughtering young men he encountered became a re-enactment of a terrible dream in which his father was slaughtering him when he was a boy.

Meanwhile, law-enforcement investigators in Texas were waking up to the fact that a probable serial killer was on the loose and this meant they would need the help of the nation's biggest criminal investigative machine to track him across North America and bring him to justice.

It was time to call in the FBI.

18

'The overall mission of the FBI is to uphold the law through the investigation of violations of federal criminal statutes, to protect the United States from hostile intelligence efforts, to provide assistance to other federal, state and local law-enforcement agencies, and to perform those responsibilities in a manner that is faithful to the Constitution and laws of the United States.'

– FBI Mission Statement

The J Edgar Hoover Building sits on a block of prime real estate, halfway between the White House and Capitol Hill on Pennsylvania Avenue, in Washington, DC. A vast, cream-coloured, multi-storey monster, it can easily lay claim to being the city's ugliest building. It also happens to be the national headquarters of the Federal Bureau of Investigation, the most powerful law-enforcement agency on earth.

For almost 70 years, America has been bombarded with movies, TV shows, books and articles devoted to the FBI's activities. The bureau is entrenched in this nation's mythology.

And within the FBI there is a culture of secrecy that still exists even today. Many in the bureau would prefer not to be accountable to the public. But the reality is that the FBI is accountable like every other law-enforcement agency.

The FBI is the principal investigative arm of the Department of Justice of the United States. The bureau spends most of its time investigating persons or incidents where there is a reason to believe that a crime has been committed or is likely to be committed.

All of the FBI's senior executives, with the exception of the director, work out of FBI headquarters. Then there are the 8,000 people who provide the bureau's field operations.

It was the field office in Houston that was about to take charge of the hunt for 'Rafael Resendez-Ramirez' as he was still known to law-enforcement personnel at the time. Almost all the FBI's day-to-day operations are carried out through those 56 field offices and another 400 satellite resident agencies.

Field agents are renowned for having far fewer illusions about the organisation and being more cynical about the FBI bureaucracy.

It is out in the field where careers are made and lost, where reputations are built and destroyed.

~

The Houston field office – with more than 200 personnel – covers much of south Texas and, with its satellite resident agencies, is responsible for a track of land bigger than most European countries.

As in every FBI office around the country, agents are assigned according to the investigative priorities established by the special agent in charge. At Houston, this was Don C Clark.

Although Clark keeps many of his agents in the usual investigative categories – counterintelligence, counterterrorism, organised crime and public corruption – his main priorities broadly reflect the two most serious problems associated with this part of Texas, white-collar crime and violent crime. Both have their roots in the roller-coaster Texan economy of the past 30 years.

Houston has always been a violent city, just as Texas has always been a violent state. The right to bear arms has always been taken seriously in the Lone Star state – many believe it has something to do with a frontier attitude.

As problems with violent crimes in the 1980s grew, the state's jail system filled to capacity. That was when the FBI stepped in to help investigate homicides, larcenies, thefts and robberies that had in the past remained the preserve of local and state police. However, once those violent crimes crossed state lines, then they came under FBI jurisdiction.

Houston chief Don C Clark has been called many things in his time, but a 'typical FBI agent' is not one of them. He worked his own way and was renowned for getting results in Houston. He was working under this principle in June 1999 when he found himself contemplating the murderous habits of one 'Rafael Resendez-Ramirez'.

~

On 9 June 1999, the FBI announced they were launching 'Operation Stop Train' – a dramatic title that seemed certain to send everyone in the country who lived near a railway into a state of blind panic.

The bureau would be spearheading a force to track down alleged Railway Killer Rafael Resendez-Ramirez, the man investigators had dubbed a 'career criminal', responsible for bludgeoning to death at least five people.

Don Clark made the FBI offices in Houston the clearing house for all local, state and federal investigators searching for 'Resendez-Ramirez', as they still continued to call him.

'Clearly, we need to talk to him,' announced Tela Mange, spokeswoman for the Texas Department of Public Safety in a classic piece of understatement. 'I would consider him to be very dangerous. This is an extremely violent way to kill someone. We're focusing on the clues he's left behind to figure out where he is, and talking with anyone we think might be able to give us information on his whereabouts.'

The FBI issued a holding charge against Angel Resendez of unlawful flight to avoid prosecution for allegedly burgling the home of Dr Claudia Benson, killed on 17 December 1998.

In Fayette County, Texas, where Angel was alleged to have killed Josephine Konvicka, investigators announced, 'We're running day and night checking on sightings, but there have been none of any substance yet.'

But they admitted, 'We feel sorry for any Hispanic male walking along the road right now... People around here are used to living with their doors, windows and cars unlocked. But there's fear down here now, I'll be frank with you. Our gun stores have all sold out of their weapons.'

During a series of meetings at the FBI field offices in Houston, lawmen compared notes and theories as to why one suspect had struck such disparate victims.

Afterwards, one investigator admitted, 'We have no pre-planned motive. I don't believe he's stalking these people, or that he's out for money. When he breaks into these homes, I don't believe he has a clue who's in there. I think he just jumps off the train and goes to the first house he can get into.'

The FBI publicly labelled Angel Resendez as an intelligent, methodical killer who enjoyed slaying his victims. That may well have inadvertently helped improve his chances of staying free because people who encountered him recalled he was anything but sophisticated-looking. People were on the lookout for the wrong kind of man.

Back in Rodeo, Mexico, Angel Resendez also gave the opposite impression to his family and friends.

And gradually some experts began questioning the

FBI pronouncements. Former bureau profiler and press analyst John Douglas – whose old unit, the National Centre for the Analysis of Violent Crime, was assisting the Houston-based FBI task force – insisted that the man now known throughout North America as 'The Railway Killer' was nothing more than a sloppy opportunist loser whose frustration with life had spilled over into violent rage. 'He's just a careless, bungling crook. He's very disorganised,' said Douglas.

Douglas – a pioneer in the science of getting inside the criminal mind – had authored several books on the subject so his opinions were highly respected. Douglas even outlined what he believed was the criminal background of the man suspected of being the Railway Killer.

'He probably started killing somewhere in his late twenties,' explained Douglas. 'He may have killed people like himself initially – male transients. Generally what happens to these guys is that a precipitating event in their lives pushes them to finally commit the crime – rejection from women, problems in their personal life, his job, money. The older they get the more frustrated and angry they become, but it's displaced anger.

'He's reached a level here where he's nothing. He's been a big loser; nobody wants anything to do with him,' said Douglas. 'He's angry with himself, angry at others – but not at a specific person, at the population at large.

'What America represents here is this wealthy country where he keeps getting kicked out and comes back and may try to get going in a job but just can't make ends meet. Coupled with these feelings, these inadequacies, fuelled by the fact that he's known to take alcohol, take drugs, lower his inhibitions now to go out and kill.'

Douglas reckoned that Angel Resendez was very different from the so-called traditional serial killers such as Ted Bundy and David Berkowitz, who were on a mission to seek out a particular type of person. 'Rasendez-Ramirez is haphazard, striking because his victims are key to his survival.'

Douglas added, 'He is targeting people because they have something he needs. He needs a place to hole up for the night, he needs money, alcohol and drugs.

'Certainly in some cases there's a sexual component where he's raped women close to his own age, but in other cases it's a criminal enterprise where he needs something. The sex is secondary.'

Douglas branded Angel Resendez as a serial spree killer who was not looking for attention but couldn't stop killing.

At that time, it was still not publicly known that Angel had been having sex with some of his younger female victims *after* their death.

Angel's other distinctive 'signature' left behind at each killing was the strange wall markings. But investigators at that time refused to reveal such details to prevent copycats.

The FBI believed that Angel's experience as a burglar had enabled him to locate and size up appropriate victims. They were convinced that, when Angel hitched a ride on a freight train, he didn't necessarily know where the train was heading. But, by the time he got off, with his background as a burglar, he was able to survey the area and then head for a house where he presumed there wouldn't be anyone to pose a real threat, like a big dog or a young male. He was expert at entering a home with a cutting glass and reaching in carefully to release locks.

The FBI also had evidence to suggest that Angel Resendez made a point of looking through the windows to see who was inside before breaking in. After all he was only five-foot-seven. A small man by anyone's standards. All the early weapons he used were primarily blunt-force trauma weapons – classic weapons of opportunity found at scenes. That was why he was so careful to case them out and make sure he could put himself in a definite no-lose situation.

Experts later surmised that the blunt-force trauma allegedly inflicted by Angel was so excessive it was almost an overkill. The reason was simple – he was so angry at someone he didn't even know. The key to that anger seemed to be the way his intended victim responded to him. And of course he was also trying to ensure that no witnesses survived to identify him later.

Besides labelling him sloppy and careless, criminal profiler John Douglas believed that Angel's state of desperation was likely to worsen. 'In a fugitive status with a lot of pressure on him, he'd have difficulty coping, difficulty sleeping, drinking more, and become more of a risk-taker.'

But Douglas rejected any claims that Angel Resendez was looking to get caught. 'That's ludicrous. They don't want to get caught. This guy particularly – that's what bothers him. He's been in jail before.'

Douglas and others ominously predicted further violence when authorities eventually moved in on him. 'When law enforcement finally catches him, if they corner him and he still has a handgun or some weapon, he will probably put himself in a position to take himself out,' said Douglas. 'Or he'll put himself in a position with law enforcement where there's a shootout and he dies in a blaze of glory, or dies in a situation called suicide by cop.'

~

The manhunt for Angel Resendez was immediately hampered by the lack of a co-ordinated computer system that would allow law-enforcement officials across the nation to compare notes instantly and determine the killer's pattern of behaviour. And there were differing opinions on where to concentrate on trying to find the fugitive.

Many experts urged the police and FBI to continue hunting the railway lines Angel had travelled for years. Investigators also knew they had to try and find some allies among Angel's relatives on both sides of the border.

Behind the scenes, the FBI and the Texas Rangers carefully checked toll records to see if Angel had been making phone calls to his friends and relatives in the US.

They worked on the theory that, despite being a loner, Angel needed some kind of support system. Authorities were convinced he would gravitate to the communities with the highest number of Hispanic residents.

Operation Stop Train team member Drew Carter was the investigator who began making contact with every relative he could track down across the US and Mexico. Carter – a 32-year-old Texas Ranger with just one year in the service under his belt – told the relatives he traced, 'If he calls you again, offer shelter and protection and be sympathetic.'

Carter knew full well that Angel had no back-up army of fellow criminals who would hide him underground for the rest of his life, and he was well aware that the $125,000 reward now being offered might easily tempt any of his family and friends back in Mexico to turn him in.

Meanwhile, the public across the US was growing increasingly fearful that the man now openly labelled the 'Railway Killer' might strike next in their backyard.

In the past, most serial killers had stuck to similar types of victims, such as prostitutes, runaways or women with a particular colour of hair. That meant some people could sit back and presume they wouldn't be the next victim. But the Railway Killer didn't seem to care. With the Railway Killer, *everyone* was a potential victim. Anyone of any age, colour or sex living within a short walking distance of railway tracks, particularly in locations where he'd killed before, was at risk.

The FBI task force gradually disclosed more clues about Angel Resendez that were supposed to help track him down. The bureau informed news media that he was clean shaven, wore prescription glasses and commonly worked as a day labourer or migrant worker. They also added that he was trained as an auto mechanic and was allergic to aspirin. There was also mention of Angel's numerous scars on his left wrist, forehead and his right ring finger, plus the tattoos of a snake and a flower.

'He should be considered armed and extremely dangerous. Anyone who sees him should contact their nearest law-enforcement agency or the FBI command centre in Houston,' said one FBI official.

But, for the moment, Angel Resendez seemed to have yet again disappeared into thin air.

19

On the morning of 12 June, Rodeo traffic cop Roberto Gandara nearly gave Angel a ticket for illegally parking his car in the town square. But he let him off with a warning after the two men enjoyed a warm conversation.

Not long afterwards, Angel encountered another local cop, Rodolfo Ramirez Ceniceros. Once again, he politely passed the time briefly with the officer and then calmly went back to his taco and began avidly reading the newspaper.

Seconds later, Angel stopped in the middle of both actions.

Abruptly, he folded the paper, paid his bill and took off. Inside the newspaper that day was the first local article about a man named as Rafael Resendez-Ramirez – the maniac they were calling the Railway Killer.

News of the murders had finally reached the hometown of the man most of the United States was on the alert for. But, by putting what they thought at the time was his most commonly used name, Rafael Resendez-Ramirez, in bold type above all his aliases, authorities actually gave him extra time to slip away. It wasn't until mugshot photos came out on satellite television that anyone in Rodeo even suspected that the fugitive in question was Angel Resendez.

That same night, Angel's common-law wife Julieta cooked a huge pan of meat and rice for dinner. Angel uncorked a bottle of red wine and the couple enjoyed a peaceful meal out on the porch overlooking the street where they lived.

When they finished, the couple sat and watched the sun set as Angel gently massaged Julieta's legs and back just as he had done throughout her pregnancy.

The following morning, Angel took an unexpected phone call. Julieta noticed that he spent a long time just listening to what the caller was saying. His replies were peppered with the occasional 'si' but little else.

In fact, someone was telling him that teams of American bounty hunters were on their way to Rodeo to bring him north of the border – dead or alive. It seemed a lot of people were interested in claiming that $125,000 reward money. The news sent a shiver up Angel's spine. He also knew that the FBI and their associates would not be far behind.

After he hung up the phone, Angel looked extremely

worried. He sat Julieta down and told her he would have to leave the house immediately. 'I have a problem,' he told her.

Angel took little Liria from her mother and hugged her tight.

Then Julieta noticed tears flowing down Angel's cheeks. He looked up at her and tried to wipe the dampness away but his eyes were so watered they glistened like mirrors in the early-morning sunlight.

Angel told Julieta he was being pursued by bad men but he did not explain why or by whom. He also refused to say who had called him on the telephone.

'It's better to run. I cannot stand prison. They're after me and I have no choice. If they find me, let them kill me,' he told Julieta.

She only thought about what his words really meant after he had gone.

Julieta began shaking as she watched Angel walk out of the front door.

She later recalled, 'I could not imagine how serious a problem he had. But it was as if worms were consuming his spirit from the inside.'

Julieta had always been aware of some element of darkness in her husband. He'd always seemed a lonely man without the support of his family, but she had no idea of the dreadful secrets he was hiding from her. Angel's happiness with Julieta had seemed to overcome all his inner fears and tribulations. Or so Julieta had thought.

Julieta recognised no clues of a fugitive who had

become almost a mythical figure, a brazen bogeyman able to move and strike at will. It just didn't sound like her quiet, unassuming Angel.

But, as Angel Resendez left Rodeo, that omnipresent instinct to kill was still burning a hole in his soul.

~

Anticipation and traces of frustration soon flickered across the faces of FBI investigators and Operation Stop Train support staff manning their stations in the Special Operations Centre inside the Houston FBI field office.

Task force chief Don C. Clark stood and shook hands with each investigator who every day entered the austere room filled with grey and black lock-together furniture. It had a 24-hour hub of hushed conversations, constantly ringing telephones and occasional high-level strategy meetings in a side office. But, despite Clark's relaxed demeanour, they all knew they were nowhere near tracking down their man.

In the office an easel held a large map of the Rodeo area, which was dotted with red and yellow stickers. On the corkboard lining one wall, three large colour blowups of the latest photos of Angel stared out into the room. On another wall, two large maps of the US were pinpointed with the locations of body and vehicle recovery sites. Next to these was a chart detailing similarities among the homicides.

After days of sensitive negotiation with Mexican authorities, the task force had only just gained permission to cross the border in pursuit of their man.

But it was already too late.

~

Surveillance on Angel's home in Rodeo began two days after he disappeared from the town.

Two task force investigators kept watch on his house from a rental car while the other officer – Texas Ranger Drew Carter – made discreet enquiries in the town about the man known as Angel Resendez.

The first day yielded few clues as to his whereabouts. But just about everyone in Rodeo knew all about the well-dressed *gringos* sitting in their sparkling-clean rental car.

All three investigators knew perfectly well that only a complete fool would return home in the middle of one of the biggest manhunts in criminal history.

Within 24 hours it was clear to the task force members that their surveillance would not help locate Angel – and could end up completely alienating the residents of Rodeo.

Texas Ranger Drew Carter volunteered to visit Angel's common-law wife Julieta openly to ask her for her help in locating the father of her baby daughter.

The FBI warned Carter that the plan might backfire because Angel's wife and his other relatives would probably tell him of the authorities' movements which would help him keep one step ahead of his pursuers.

But Carter believed they had nothing to lose since the task force still had no idea where Angel was. Carter was convinced that Angel Resendez would have to contact his family eventually. In any case, they were the only direct link with the man suspected of being the notorious Railway Killer.

And his training as a Texas Ranger had encouraged him to take that sort of decision without consultation.

~

The involvement of the Texas Rangers in the hunt for Angel was a significant element because they were a specific force of investigators renowned on both sides of the border.

The old-time reputation of Texas Rangers as trigger-happy lawmen roaming Texas cattle country, camping out on remote sites close to the Rio Grande, and keeping an eye on the early oil fields is long gone. Certainly the Rangers are still in the business of hunting down bandits, rustlers and outlaws but these days they have to show the same sort of restraint as all other law-enforcement agencies.

However, the Rangers still manage to preserve their individuality. All of them are renowned as showing great initiative and originality of thought. They are truly proud of the title and always refer to the Rangers as 'the service' and never as 'the force'. Over the years, imported efficiency experts who don't appreciate the Rangers' traditions have tried to turn them into just another police force. But they have always steadfastly refused to drop their title.

The Ranger Service, probably more than any other

organisation, has always remained dependent on the quality of its personnel. As one old-timer once said, 'We'd rather have a good man armed with a muzzle loader than a poor one armed with a machine gun.'

While fingerprinting, ballistics and a vast range of other scientific methods of crime detection have become an essential part of law enforcement, there is no doubt that the very title 'Texas Ranger' gives an investigator an edge over any other policeman. There is something in the name 'Ranger' that makes the wildest cowboy completely dedicated the moment he puts on that hat.

And even today it is recognised that any Ranger commander who fails to make full use of these traditions is likely to fail to inspire his men.

Charged with enforcing laws, quelling riots, investigating major crimes and catching fugitives, the Rangers work in large areas on their own. That independence and tough competition for each Ranger job has helped colour their image as steely, laconic cowboy heroes.

In the early days of the corps, however, that same stamp of autonomy made many Latinos fearful of crossing paths with the Rangers.

When the Rangers were formed in 1823, Texas was still part of Mexico. The original Rangers were 10 volunteers summoned by Texas founding father Stephen F Austin to protect white settlers.

Twelve years later, Texas's new provisional government formalised the group as a frontier defence force against Native Americans and Mexicans.

In the chaotic aftermath of the Civil War, the state legislature created two Ranger forces to control 'marauding or thieving parties' in the still contested frontier zone. In 1901, a law was passed permitting the governor to create his own Ranger force in the region. The men performed their duties with minimal supervision and ferocious dispatch, mounting cross-border raids that included massacres of Mexicans remembered to this day in the form of *corridos* – story songs – and children's tales of 'los Rinches', bloodthirsty Rangers who snatch and kill children.

But, side-by-side with the resentment and fear, another, more enduring Ranger mystique developed. It is something that has remained with them to this day.

As Texas Department of Public Safety spokesman Mike Cox says, 'There were bloody raids into Texas from Mexico, and there were bloody retaliations on the part of local citizens as well as Texas Rangers.

'But that was then, this is now. The Ranger ethic used to be: "Shoot first, ask questions later." These days it's: "Ask questions first and shoot only if you have to."'

Today, the force consists[Q? **Going into the new millennium, the force consisted**] of 107 officers and is diverse. It includes five black men, 14 Latino men, one Asian man and two women, one white and one black.

To some Latinos on both sides of the border, the Rangers may have been a tad brutal in the past but they were an independent, strong-willed organisation, which made them more trustworthy than the regular law-enforcement agencies.

'Years ago, they didn't do right by Hispanics in general,' recalled San Antonio defence lawyer Jesse Gamas. 'But I think the new era of Texas Rangers has a higher-than-average reputation among everybody. Every community that I know in Texas, when there's a problem, they call the Rangers.'

That air of straight-shooting, cowboy autonomy earned them respect even among criminals in the border areas.

And, during his 20-odd years hopping trains and criss-crossing that same border, Angel Resendez had heard about the Rangers' reputation. Many said they were a force to be reckoned with. Angel Resendez had learned how to weave and work his way through the system of border control and law enforcement, to work trains, to get through *garitas* or border checkpoints.

He believed he was good at what he did. And since the Rangers were the toughest of the tough then at least they qualified for his respect.

20

Back in Rodeo, Angel's girlfriend Julieta was understandably confused and upset when Ranger Drew Carter called at her home on that hot June afternoon.

'We've been living together for five years and I had no idea about this,' she told Carter and two colleagues as she held their baby Liria on her lap. 'He was never violent or sadistic. He was always a real gentleman to me.'

When the agents outlined the evidence they had which linked her husband to at least eight murders, she looked at them very seriously and said, 'If he did what you are saying, his spirit is rotting and his mind must be disturbed.'

She admitted that the man she called 'my Angel' had said he would run because there was no choice. Carter and his law-enforcement colleagues collected a bundle of Angel's clothing, his bike and his guitar for forensic tests.

But it was when Julieta passed over paycheque stubs and more than 100 pieces of jewellery that would later be directly linked to many of Angel's victims that the full enormity of her lover's crimes sunk in.

Julieta broke down in front of the agents. 'You don't know what's inside a man's head. But we were a very stable couple.'

Looking around at the sheer normality of the home Julieta had shared with Angel, Carter and his two colleagues knew what she meant.

That day – for the first time in eight years – Julieta missed a day at work at Rodeo's public health clinic. She had already stopped eating since Angel had walked out a few days earlier.

Ranger Drew Carter knew it wouldn't be easy. He was about to lay his cards on the table – and that meant convincing Angel's family that their gentle, caring Angel was a vicious, cold-blooded murderer of complete strangers.

FBI Special Agent Rolando Moss was also present at the meeting with Julieta. He later explained, 'It was as big a surprise to her as anybody.'

Moss never forgot the expression on the face of Julieta. It was, he later said, a twisted combination of trauma, distress and frustration.

'Is this the man I have been married to?' she asked the investigators incredulously.

They nodded their heads slowly and almost apologetically.

Julieta tried to help the task force. But the investigators

present remained convinced that Julieta still hadn't completely grasped the enormity of what Angel had done.

'She was in complete and utter shock,' recalled Moss.

One of the few details Julieta did discuss was that Angel's sister Manuela Maturino – who lived across the border in Albuquerque – was the one relative he stayed in close contact with throughout his travels. Ranger Carter felt that maybe Angel's sister could be the link that might eventually lead to the man most of the America wanted behind bars as speedily as possible.

It had to be worth a try.

Carter convinced his bosses the key to tracking down Angel Resendez was to keep building on those ongoing relationships with his relatives, especially the ones he regularly visited in the United States.

At the end of June, Carter made contact with Angel's sister at her home in Albuquerque.

Carter's big advantage was that the Rangers' unusual personal autonomy in decision-making meant it was easier for him to just go ahead and get things done. Carter perfectly fitted the Texas Ranger criteria of being someone who could stand on his own two feet and didn't have to run everything he did past a supervisor.

To some of Angel Resendez's relatives, Carter already seemed a much more honourable man than most of the other *gringos* who'd come knocking on their doors in recent weeks.

But, as if to illustrate this problem, Angel's 'Most Wanted' poster was torn down from the wall of Rodeo's only drugstore within two days of being nailed up.

As brief details of Angel's background filtered through to the nation's press media, dozens of reporters made the trek to Rodeo to find out more about the so-called Railway Killer's 'other life'. Journalists were warned by Mexican Police to be careful, as strangers were not greeted with open arms in Rodeo.

Reporters soon concluded that harbouring a wanted criminal was not difficult in a place like Rodeo.

'It's the sort of town where they know who you are before you check in the local motel,' said one seasoned campaigner after a two-day visit to Rodeo.

And the few local people who talked to journalists made Angel sound more like a saint than a serial killer.

Bricklayer Eduardo Buceaga Perez, 60, was building a house on a lot owned by Angel. He told one reporter, 'He seems like good people, but who knows what he has in his heart.'

And one of the town's cops insisted that the couple largely kept to themselves. 'He doesn't have any friends. He never talks to anyone.'

The FBI and half of America believed Angel Resendez was a heavy drug and alcohol abuser, always armed with at least one handgun. But in Rodeo no one would even admit to having seen Angel in a local *cantina*. He also had no local police record and there was no sign of his love of guns either.

Local cafe owner Mama Moreno refused to even believe that Angel had committed any crimes. 'From the behaviour that he has when he is here... I don't think so.'

Julieta told one visiting reporter, 'My Angel loved his daughter almost too much. He kept saying how she was so beautiful.'

Everyone who met little Liria noted that she had a shock of thick dark hair, and certain facial expressions made her closely resemble her fugitive father, whose photo was by now in every newspaper and on every TV screen in North America.

'Innocence is redemption,' Julieta told a journalist with tears welling up in her eyes. 'But the baby is the most important thing.'

~

Meanwhile, Angel Resendez was back in the US, travelling by train back up towards the Midwest.

Merely the sight of a comfortable house near the tracks aroused a frenzy of complex feelings within Angel. Being hunted down by half of America made Angel feel even more rejected by the country he had used and abused so often.

Angel already hated Americans and everything they represented. But another side of him wished he was American so he could lead a normal life and get off those railway tracks for good. But now the two conflicting emotions had intertwined to become one.

He now felt the urge once again to destroy another

American's life. To destroy the power that had rejected him and forced him to lead a hobo's life hopping the railways. Those disturbing memories of prison also accelerated his hatred.

All this combined to become the fatal tripwire for the segment of Angel's out-of-control brain.

These feelings created a rush to his head. He'd look out from the train car he was sitting in and see a big house out on the horizon, standing isolated. Within minutes, he'd jump the freight train and march single-mindedly across the streets in search of revenge.

That emotional force was building and building in his brain and spiralling to impel him to his next atrocity. It would just take a few angry blows to render his victim helpless.

On 15 June 1999, officials in the small town of Gorham, in Jackson County, Illinois, found the bodies of residents George Morber, Sr, 80, and his daughter, Carolyn Frederick, 52, slain during the night in Morber's mobile home next to a rail line.

The intruder had shot Morber in the head with his own shotgun. Then he'd beaten Frederick to death with the back of the weapon before committing a sexual act. There was also clear evidence that the killer had stayed in the house some time after the murders because he appeared to have helped himself to food from the kitchen. Morber's red Chevrolet pickup truck was missing.

Sheriff William Kilquist, in charge of the investigation, had no doubt the killer was 'someone who had done it before'. He explained, 'I was on the scene within 45 minutes of it being reported, and it was obvious that whoever did it had done it before. It was not a lark or a casual thing.'

On 16 June, a witness in Cairo, Illinois, on the junction of the Mississippi and Ohio rivers saw Angel Resendez dropping off the missing Chevrolet pickup truck he stole from victim George Morber's home in Gorham, 60 miles to the north. Angel was said by authorities to be wearing a white shirt, blue jeans and a brown baseball cap with the letter 'T' in the centre.

Later that same day, Angel was seen at two homeless shelters dressed in the same clothes.

At first, local law-enforcement officials were reluctant to connect the double slaying to the Railway Killer.

Jackson County's State Attorney Michael Wepsiec told reporters, 'I can't say if he is a suspect or if he isn't. At this point in time, we do not have fingerprints or DNA. The crime lab is processing any evidence right now to see if it compares.'

Two days later the FBI publicly announced that Angel Resendez was the number-one suspect in the double killings of George Morber and his daughter Carolyn.

The bureau – now openly spearheading the local, state and federal task force to track down the Railway Killer – also finally conceded that they were about to place Angel Resendez at the head of the agency's Most Wanted list.

The APB internet site summed up the situation by saying, 'Authorities say the 39-year-old Mexican national bludgeoned six people to death with whatever was at hand, usually during a night-time burglary. They say fingerprints and other forensic evidence tie him to all six killings.

'All of the attacks occurred near railway tracks. The five-foot-seven-inch, 150-pound Resendez-Ramirez, whose criminal record spans more than 20 years, hitched a ride aboard a freight train to first enter the United States in 1976 and has been riding the rails ever since, officials at the US Immigration and Naturalization Service (INS) said.'

On Thursday, 17 June, the Associated Press reported that police in Houston had arrested a man they said could be the Railway Killer. The agency stated, 'The Department of Public Safety and Round Rock Police arrested five people on a freight train in Williamson County, one of whom may be Rafael Resendez-Ramirez,' DPS spokesman Mike Cox was quoted as saying.

But within hours the AP were retracting the report after another DPS spokesman Tom Vingar said, 'Hope is fading fast that it's Rafael Resendez-Ramirez. The man who was arrested bears quite a bit of a resemblance to him. Everybody got a little bit overexcited.'

In Dallas, a terrified woman flagged down a police cruiser after claiming she'd seen a man answering the Railway Killer's description lurking around a dilapidated guesthouse.

Dozens of police were on the scene within minutes but when they raided the house they ended up finding 40 undocumented immigrants hiding in the dank basement of the property – but there was no sign of the man named as a suspected serial killer.

In New Braunfels, Texas, police thought they'd come across another of Angel's victims when they found the body of an elderly man in an apartment complex next to railway tracks.

But within minutes of the Houston Police Department and Texas Rangers arriving on the scene it was established that their man was not involved.

Back in Houston; a man was travelling in his car with his elderly mother on a sunny day at the end of June when he was stopped by a man asking him for a ride.

His mother refused – believing the man was Mexican – and possibly the fugitive.

'She didn't say no until she turned around and saw he was Mexican,' the man later recalled. 'I really wasn't worried about it. She overreacted.'

Meanwhile, investigators throughout Texas regularly stopped freight trains in the search for Angel.

In Round Rock, Texas, police arrested a Mexican national on an eastbound Union Pacific freight train only to discover he was not their man.

At the same time, police found five Hispanic men hiding beneath a shipment of tyres. One of them even had a snake tattoo on his arm – just like Angel. But the tattoo was on the wrong arm.

All five Hispanic men were undocumented aliens and

were charged with trespassing. They were put in the Williamson County Jail.

'I think some people got a little excited there at first but what are you going to do? You've just got to act,' Vingar added.

Just a few hours later, police in Houston announced publicly for the first time they had finally identified Angel's fingerprint inside the 1993 Honda Civic owned by his schoolteacher victim Noemi Dominguez.

On a sleepy Sunday morning in the Illinois town of Percy, grandmother Donna McHughes, 58, was driving to her local Laundromat. She'd read all about alleged serial killer 'Rafael Resendez-Ramirez' in her local paper after the awful murder of an 80-year-old man and his 52-year-old daughter in the town of Gorham, 20 miles to the west. But she wasn't worried, as the papers had said the killer had hopped a train and was most likely hundreds of miles away before the crime had even been discovered.

A few minutes later, Donna was all alone in the Laundromat busily pushing all her washing into the machine when she became aware of someone looking over at her. She looked up at the clock on the wall – it was 8.30 am.

She slowly straightened herself up from the washing machine and turned her head towards the window. Donna later recalled, 'They say death has many faces but for me it will always be his twisted face. I could see his cold, black eyes staring at me through the glass of the Laundromat window.'

Donna immediately recognised there was something wrong with the man. The way he stared at her gave her the creeps. His face was contorted into a kind of twisted mask of hatred and his eyes were flat, dark, without expression.

For a few seconds Donna was rooted to the spot. She stared back at the man, too terrified to even take a breath.

Then the man moved from the window and started walking towards the front door of the Laundromat.

A voice inside her urged her: 'Get out! Get out!'

She left her laundry and her change on the washing machine, and walked slowly towards the back door of the Laundromat.

Donna kept telling herself, 'Don't run, Donna. If you do, he'll chase you.'

When she reached the door, she threw it open and ran to her car, jumped inside it and immediately started it up and screeched out of the parking lot at high speed.

Donna didn't stop until she reached a local convenience store a few blocks away. Close to tears, she told the woman behind the counter what had happened.

Then she dashed to a phone and called her son Kevin, a sheriff's deputy in a neighbouring county. He immediately alerted the local police.

When investigators arrived they showed Donna a photo of Angel Resendez and she recognised him straight away.

'Yes, that's him. That's the guy.'

The officer replied, 'You're a very lucky woman. This is the man we want for a whole string of murders. He was probably stalking you. You were probably going to be his next victim.'

Donna trembled when she heard him say that. She later recalled, 'I just about died with shock.'

Her son told her that her face went as white as a sheet. That night Donna was so scared she stayed with her sister in the nearby town of Sparta. She didn't sleep a wink and sometime before dawn she burst into tears and couldn't stop crying 'when it suddenly hit me how close I'd come to ending up like that poor old man in Gorham and his daughter. That could have been me. I believe with all my heart that voice telling me to get out of that Laundromat was the voice of an angel sent by God.'

~

Angel's alleged slaying of George Morber and his daughter Carolyn in Illinois introduced a whole new part of the country to his brand of random murder. Sightings in Kentucky had also confirmed the FBI's worst fears – that the search efforts were now nationwide.

Meanwhile, fear among ordinary Americans was growing at an alarming rate.

Even FBI task force chief Don C. Clark conceded, 'I think he could be considered public enemy number one right now and we really need to get him off the streets.'

TV networks across the country joined in the public

outcry by cutting live to every development in the case, however small.

The Railway Killer had captured every-one's imagination.

21

Nationwide publicity about the Railway Killer provoked unbridled terror among homeowners who lived near freight train lines.

The Operation Stop Train task force conceded that, until they caught Angel, there was little they could do to allay fears that he could jump from any passing train and descend on people's nearby homes.

In Flatonia, Texas, when police stopped a long freight train and mounted a car-by-car search, it sparked yet another rumour that Angel Resendez had been caught.

'There's a lot of rumours going around, that we chased a guy down the tracks and let him go, that we had him pinned under a house. We're just trying to squash some of those,' Flatonia Police Chief Leonard Cox told local residents when he addressed 200 worried homeowners at an American Legion hall in Flatonia.

'It's got people concerned. It really does. Alarm companies had been trebling sales over the previous couple of weeks.'

Over at West University Place, Houston, Police Chief Gary Bryce, who'd linked Angel to the slaying of Dr Claudia Benton the previous December, said, 'We have never been exposed to anything like this. He's an extremely dangerous man who's shown he can be extremely brutal, and he needs to be caught.'

During the previous few weeks, the Texas Department of Safety (DPS), Houston FBI and other investigators had fielded dozens of calls from police nationwide looking to compare notes and evidence from their own unsolved murders, especially those that involved bludgeoning.

Behind the scenes, numerous police forces were putting pressure on the FBI to place Angel Resendez on its Ten Most Wanted list. But the bureau was worried that, if they released too much information about their suspect, he might never return from Mexico.

'If you give out a lot of information, that also makes prosecutions difficult,' explained one FBI source at the time. 'And it makes it easy for a lot of copycats.'

However, the task force now knew that another slaying in northeast Texas was being linked to Angel so the pressure to step up the manhunt was growing.

In the small town of Hughes Springs, friends had found resident Leafie Mason, 87, beaten to death on 2 October 1998.

The victim also lived near railway tracks. A night-time intruder had apparently entered her house through an unlocked window. Investigators were almost certain the killing had been committed by 'Rafael Resendez-Ramirez'.

Meanwhile, the border patrol and other investigators continued to stop and search passing trains – sparking even more false reports of Railway Killer sightings.

One anonymous phone tip from a resident of Austin, Texas, provoked officers to arrest five illegal immigrants on an eastbound freight train. But none of them turned out to be the wanted killer.

The INS – still embarrassed by their failure to detain Angel on 2 June– admitted a San Antonio woman had reported seeing a man answering Angel's description lurking near a house along the city's Chicago Boulevard. But, as Ray Dudley, spokesman for the INS's San Antonio District, later conceded. 'That kind of gossip in any neighbourhood scares the heck out of people.'

Many experienced law-enforcement investigators admit that when a serial killer is being hunted in a high-profile case a lot of other 'small-timers' can literally get away with murder.

'The problem is everyone wants to blame the serial killer for any unsolved homicide so police can clear up their books,' explained one OST member. 'I reckon there's hundreds of one-off killers out there who've got away scot-free 'cause some mass killer has been blamed for a murder they committed.'

Near Galina, in Illinois, just a couple of days after

Angel had allegedly killed the father and daughter in nearby Gorham, another couple were found shot dead in their rented farmhouse just a few feet from the local freight train line.

Not so surprisingly, investigators immediately suspected that Angel was responsible. Apple River (population 400) residents Darin J Oellerich, 23, and his fiancée Rhonda Sue Wurm, 25, seemed to perfectly fit the profile of his previous victims.

But two days later deputies arrested a local man and Angel was immediately eliminated as a suspect in the double slaying.

District Attorney Don Schweihs explained, 'Mr Ramirez has been excluded from the case. There is no reason to believe he was ever in the area. People can rest assured there is not a killer on the loose.'

Over in nearby Pontiac, investigators were similarly convinced they'd found another of Angel's victims following the death of a 40-year-old woman, Juanita Sapp.

One of Sapp's neighbours in her Lincolnshire apartment complex had found her body in bushes outside her home on the morning of 16 June.

Pontiac Police Chief Don Schlosser tried to play down the connection by telling newsmen at the scene, 'That's just one of the many points we're checking into. We have not positively linked him yet.'

Chief Schlosser would not release the exact cause of death but admitted the killing was 'not the result of a firearm incident'. He added, 'Every police agency in the Midwest is watching for this guy. If he's out and visible, someone will spot him.'

Significantly, Tom Vingar, spokesman for the Texas Department of Public Safety, quickly issued a statement saying that investigators on the federal task force hunting for Angel did not believe the Sapp slaying fit his pattern of killing.

On 20 June 1999, police in Jackson County, Illinois, matched Angel's fingerprints found at the scene of the Gorham killings.

The following day at the Jackson County, Illinois, circuit court, an arrest warrant was issued for 'Rafael Resendez-Ramirez, aka Pedro Jaramarillo', charging him with first-degree murder and home invasion.

Bail was set at $1 million but the main aim of the warrant was to let Angel know that he was going to be made to pay for every single crime he was suspected of committing.

~

On 21 June 1999, FBI Director Louis J Freeh finally announced the placement of 'Rafael Resendez-Ramirez' on the bureau's Most Wanted list. They still didn't have his correct name, which would ultimately cost them time and money in the hunt for the alleged serial killer. But at least the FBI operation was now pulling out all the stops.

Director Freeh said, 'This case underscores the value of the FBI's Ten Most Wanted programme by not only alerting the public to the very real dangers posed by violent criminals to all innocent Americans, but also by serving as a key that unlocks the door to a suspect's whereabouts. We hope that the publicity afforded to Mr Ramirez today by local authorities in Texas and Illinois, as well as by this Top Ten announcement, will bring swift apprehension.'

Angel Resendez was still hopping on and off freight trains, keeping one step ahead of authorities, but he must have found it difficult to come to terms with all the attention he was causing.

~

Angel Resendez – or Rafael Resendez-Ramirez, as he was still being called – had finally been placed on top of the bureau's Ten Most Wanted Fugitives List. But would this help bring about a speedy arrest of the suspect?

The history of the FBI Most Wanted list seemed to suggest it would.

One hundred and thirty-four criminals had been apprehended as a direct result of citizens recognising them from the Most Wanted poster campaign since it was started on 14 March 1950.

The FBI's Ten Most Wanted Fugitives programme was designed to publicise the nation's most fearsome criminals, who might not otherwise get that sort of nationwide coverage. The FBI also believed that it was their own special way of acknowledging just how valuable the public were in helping track down fugitives.

The programme first started when a crime reporter on a national news agency asked the FBI for names and descriptions of the 'toughest guys' the FBI would like to capture. The story generated so much positive publicity for the bureau that legendary FBI director J Edgar Hoover launched the programme.

To qualify for the list, all 56 of the bureau's field offices have to submit candidates who are then forwarded to the FBI deputy director for final approval.

Those criteria are.

1. The individual must have a lengthy record of committing serious crimes and/or be considered a particularly dangerous menace to society due to current criminal charges.

2. Nationwide publicity would definitely help apprehend the fugitive, who cannot already be notorious due to other publicity.

And fugitives could only be removed from the list if.

1. They were captured.

2. All charges against them were dropped

3. They no longer fit the Ten Most Wanted criteria.

The FBI themselves admit that the makeup of fugitives has changed enormously over the years. In the early days, the list was comprised mainly of bank robbers, burglars and car thieves. Once into the radical 60s, its attention turned to political revolutionaries. Then in recent years serial murderers and drug-related crimes have taken priority.

By July 1999, there had been a total of 457 fugitives

on the list. Out of that an impressive 429 had been hunted down.

The FBI's 'Seeking Information' poster could ultimately also prove just as relevant to Angel's alleged killing spree. On it were pictures of five women who'd been murdered. The chances were high that at least one of them was slain by Angel during his travels on the railway.

~

The wave of hysteria sweeping the US as the hunt for 'Rafael Resendez-Ramirez' continued reached a tragic peak on 24 June when a man shot and killed a woman on his doorstep – because he thought the person pounding and kicking his door was the alleged rail-riding serial killer.

The man fired four rounds from a semi-automatic handgun through the front door of his home on Spanish Street, in Cape Girardeau, Missouri, not realising it was his neighbour. Police later said the 44-year-old victim was intoxicated and thought she was entering her own house. She died of a gunshot wound to the head.

Cape Girardeau (population 8,000) sits just across the Mississippi River from Gorham, Illinois, where Angel was believed to have killed two people only a few days earlier.

In the days following the bizarre incident, it was unclear whether the man would face murder charges as, under Missouri law, a person can use deadly force to protect himself if he reasonably believes someone is trying to break into his home.

Local police sergeant Carl Kinnison even conceded that fear of the alleged serial killer 'certainly factors into this particular case because Spanish Street lies two blocks from a rail line'.

'Resendez-Ramirez has been spotted in several communities in the area,' added Kinnison. 'Last night, just south of here, a person was seen jumping off a train.'

In the middle of all this fear and trepidation, yet more psychological profiles of Angel were being publicised. Many insisted he had to be a sadistic man who killed his victims in order to feel invincible. But no amount of criminal profiles helped the Operation Stop Train task force get any closer to their man.

22

Angel wasn't the only hobo travelling the tracks of North America. But his alleged killing spree was giving a lot of harmless hobos a bad name, according to Buzz Potter, president of a loosely knit group called the National Hobo Association. He and many others travelling the railways for free found themselves subject to regular searches and Potter pointed out the situation had become so serious that 'anybody who sees two grimy guys at the back door would bolt the door and dial 911'.

There has never been an entirely accurate numbers of hobos available, but Union Pacific agents detained more than 97,000 people for trespassing in 1998. Most were released with nothing more than a warning.

Rail riding itself had always been associated with the Depression, but in fact the numbers of those out on the tracks in the 90s were growing by the month. And the old-time image of a homeless, rootless hobo living on handouts and camping in hobo 'jungles' alongside tracks was far from accurate these days.

Hobo leader Buzz Potter believes, 'A lot of guys who have PhDs ride freight trains. None of the guys I know would hurt a flea.'

Many adventure-seekers jumped trains armed with credit cards and train schedules out for a two-week trip. And then there were the tens of thousands of undocumented immigrants like Angel Resendez who were taking the cheapest travel option on their way to work.

However, there was another more deadly aspect to freight train hopping. In 1995, 522 people were killed in incidents involving trains throughout the US. Although this number did include suicides and pedestrians hit by trains, there was still a large number who simply died getting on and off the cars illegally. The scars all over Angel's body were a testament to that.

Duffy Littlejohn, author of *Hopping Freight Trains in America*, has ridden 500,000 miles on freight trains since 1970. But he also happens to be a lawyer living in San Luis Obispo, California.

So why did he do it? 'There's danger. There's thrill. There's risk because it's illegal,' he says. 'This is a rich, rich American tradition, riding the rails.'

To Angel – the most wanted man in America – riding the rails had simply become an economic necessity. He knew nothing of tradition. He was using the freight trains as a means to a deadly end.

Back in Texas, Angel Resendez's name was on everyone's mind and most residents' lips.

Harris County Assistant District Attorney Devon Anderson – who was looking to prosecute Angel Resendez for the slaying of Dr Claudia Benton the previous December – went out of Houston and stopped at a convenience store on Interstate 10. It had numerous photos and posters of Resendez. Every citizen and every cop seemed to be on the alert for him.

'It's so terrifying because he's getting into people's houses,' said Anderson. 'He's the real deal. He's a real-life serial killer and you don't see them very often. It's like something out of the movies.'

Over in Lexington, Kentucky, Assistant Police Chief Fran Root's enquiries into the murder of student Christopher Maier back in August 1997 were still hitting a complete brick wall despite an entry into the FBI's computerised Violent Criminal Apprehension Program. Then Root heard about Angel's alleged killings in Weimar and West University Place, Houston, and he decided to look more closely at certain similarities.

In Lulling, Texas, investigators were awaiting the result of forensic tests to determine whether Angel was responsible for killing Salvador Rojas, 31. Rojas's Mexican houseguest – who arrived by train before Thanksgiving – had been missing since Rojas was found bludgeoned to death on 30 November 1998. Back in Houston, more details about Angel's background were gradually released to the public. INS Houston district spokeswoman Luisa Aquino disclosed to journalists how Angel had first been caught entering the country illegally in August 1976, by hopping a train.

Then she gave a breakdown of his previous run-ins with the INS and added, 'He's evidently a master of coming up with different identities.'

Authorities continued painting a picture of a cunning, artful man swapping moustaches and hairstyles like the wind. The real Angel seemed a very different proposition altogether.

A few days after allegedly committing those three brutal slayings in fast succession, Angel was sighted in familiar territory – Louisville, Kentucky.

A drug-abuse counsellor out watering flowers at a local homeless shelter spoke for a few minutes to a passing man who matched his description. He said he was heading for California. It was not until later the woman realised who he was. But, as she pointed out, 'He was kind of wide-eyed and alert. He seemed really happy and cheerful.'

~

The law-enforcement officials in Lexington finally charged 'Rafael Resendez-Ramiraz' with Christopher Maier's murder and robbery and the rape of his girlfriend. They also blanketed the state with Teletypes and wallet-sized cards carrying Angel's photograph and relevant information. Many officials were convinced he was still in the state following those sightings.

Lexington police investigator Sergeant Mike Barnard even traced a number of Angel's relatives in the city and interviewed them.

Barnard refused to publicly reveal what the family members had to say but he did confirm that they were fully co-operating with police.

Barnard told reporters that he and the Operation Stop Train task force hunting Angel intended to lock down the state to prevent him from slipping away.

'We're going to send Teletypes to all police agencies in Kentucky today describing him, and we've got over 2,000 cards we're printing up with his description to get to the migrant workers in the area and get them on our side,' explained Barnard.

The task force genuinely believed they could squeeze Angel to the point where he would be forced into making a mistake. As Barnard admitted, 'We have a lot at stake here. We have the original homicide; we have the only living witness who can identify him.'

Angel's family ties and the fact he used to work the tobacco fields in Russell County convinced Kentucky authorities they could genuinely be on his trail.

'We received word that he had worked in Lexington frequently and was here to get migrant work,' added Barnard.

A picture of the most wanted man in North America was the first thing people saw when they stepped into the Hope Center's homeless outreach motor home near Lexington, Kentucky.

Plastered across telephone poles, walls, bulletin

boards and any other place they could fit them were posters bearing a face that police, both locally and nationally, hoped people would recognise if they saw it and then contact authorities.

But there was another disturbing thought in the minds of Lexington Police following those sightings of Angel Resendez. Was he returning to try and find the only living witness to his atrocities? There was a genuine fear that the assailant who had murdered Christopher Maier and left his girlfriend for dead might come back to Kentucky to complete some 'unfinished business' by wiping out the life of the one person who had met him face-to-face when he was in the process of committing homicide.

With news of the Railway Killer mentioned in every newspaper and TV programme across the nation, that girlfriend found it so disturbing that she fled abroad to avoid the rush of publicity associated to the case.

The girlfriend was, according to her mother, working hard to try and overcome the trauma caused by the horrific attack during which Angel had raped and beaten her after killing Maier.

As the net seemed at last to be closing on Angel, the woman's mother told reporters that she was 'hoping there will be enough physical evidence from the other crimes to convict him without her having to testify'.

~

News of the massive manhunt for so-caked Railway Killer Angel Resendez had spread across the world as

America's propensity for serial killers once again became a subject of great fascination.

The Times headlined their story: 'HOBO SERIAL KILLER TERRORISES TEXAS'. The paper then breathlessly informed its readers. 'A huge manhunt is under way for a hobo serial killer who travels America's railways picking off random victims.'

And *The Times* also pointed out, 'Train-hopping travellers who have always held a romanticised place in American culture may never be regarded in the same way again.'

~

But Operation Stop Train was running out of steam before it had really even got started. Investigators were working with a four-year-old photo of Angel Resendez. The FBI even admitted privately he might simply sit tight in Mexico, whose extradition treaty with the US wasn't exactly airtight, especially when it came to suspects who faced the death penalty.

There was also the continuing saga of Angel's identification. By the time the FBI established for certain that he was actually called Angel Leoncio Reyes Resendez it was, they claimed, less confusing to keep calling him Resendez-Ramirez.

But some investigators within the task force believed that this confusion over his real name was allowing the alleged Railway Killer to keep a low profile because he didn't fit the description that was being circulated.

Task force leader Don C. Clark told reporters, 'All I do

know is that, if this person is the person we suspect in these crimes, he's a very dangerous and violent person.'

As for the suspect's motive, agent Clark could only say, 'I wish I could tell you.'

In Houston, immigrant Mexicans providing cheap labour in the city claimed that freelance construction work had plummeted since the manhunt went public. As labourer Diego Xiloj explained, 'I think the employers are scared of us. As long as Resendez-Ramirez is uncaught, it's going to continue affecting us.'

Neither Xiloj nor other workers said they blamed employers for being scared, but they genuinely feared the longer he was on the run the more it could affect their ability to earn a living.

The biggest problem was caused by the fact that Angel's first-glance description was so generic – five feet, seven inches, 140 to 150 pounds, medium build.

He could have been virtually anyone – and his photos did not provide much help, either. He was so normal-looking.

23

The steel tracks glinted in the searing midday sun in front of the black and yellow Union Pacific engine as it slowly hauled its two-mile-long cargo through the sleepy city of Jackson, Mississippi.

Just then a police helicopter came swooping overhead. On the ground below, ten police cruisers screeched into the main street alongside the freight train and surged up the road until they were all well ahead of the cars.

Then two cruisers slewed across the tracks. Two policemen in black-rimmed white hats jumped out with megaphones in their hands.

'PULL UP!' they ordered. 'PULL UP!'

Three hundred yards in front of them, the driver of a massive 400-ton engine hit his brakes and the train screeched slowly to a halt.

As it did so dozens of cops, many carrying rifles and

dressed in black T-shirts, baseball caps and dark glasses, poured out of the accompanying vehicles. Three white vans pulled up behind them and more officers emerged with dogs.

The latest search operation in the hunt for Angel Resendez had begun. Across the south of America, the same scene was being repeated in dozens of locations. The nation's hunt for the Railway Killer was an ongoing drama.

Even railway companies stepped up security, watching for drifters hopping trains.

In Laredo, Texas – the busiest commercial crossing point on the US–Mexico border – agents used dogs and helicopters to root out undocumented immigrants who'd sneaked aboard freight trains headed north.

As the hunt for Angel Resendez continued, the sheer logistics of fingerprinting every immigrant hobo investigators came across on trains was solved by a laptop computer using fingerprint databases. The wonders of modern science.

'There is an urgency to this that everyone is aware of,' explained John Bromley, spokesman for Union Pacific, who revealed that ten trains were being stopped daily along routes in 23 states – double the normal number stopped.

'We stop trains every day; what's changed is that people are calling to report riders are on board,' said Bromley. 'So we are stopping trains more quickly and removing people.'

For Union Pacific, it was the first time in more than

100 years that they had been so closely involved in a manhunt. 'The last one anyone can recall was the manhunt for Jesse James,' admitted Bromley.

In Harlingen, Texas, witnesses said that the task force resembled a Wild-West-style operation as FBI, border patrol and numerous other law-enforcement agencies swooped on to a freight train.

And the Operation Stop Train task force had flooded the communities along the Railway Killer's suspected path with photos and details about Angel Resendez.

Meanwhile, serial killer profilers issued fresh warnings to the task force that their suspect was more than likely to kill again in the very near future.

As Mike Cox, spokesman for the Texas Department of Public Safety, even admitted, 'It's just a matter of time.'

The clock inside Angel Resendez's head was still ticking...

~

On 26 June, it was publicly revealed for the first time that Angel had been freed by INS border patrol officers following that routine check on 2 June. The truth came to light when the INS offered up a new photo taken of Angel when he was detained and then released by the border patrol at the beginning of June.

INS officials insisted they were unaware he was wanted for questioning in connection with at least four killings.

FBI special agent Don C. Clark even sounded embarrassed when he was asked to comment about the slip-up. 'I'm not going to discuss whether it was mechanical error or an error at all,' he said to reporters. 'I don't think it is a blow to our investigation. Clearly, we would have liked to have him right this minute. We would have liked to have him some time ago, but what it does do is give us the most current photograph we can get out to the public in hopes somebody may have seen this person.'

Neither Clark nor INS spokesman Russ Bergeron would even confirm where Angel had been picked up. Not surprisingly, press and TV pointed out that Angel had allegedly committed four more slayings following his release by the INS.

The FBI even tried to put a positive spin on the story by mentioning how they were fielding hundreds of calls every day about the fugitive killer, and it was only a matter of time before they apprehended him.

The fallout from the INS screw-up continued into the following month. INS Commissioner Doris Meissner defended her agency by pointing out they had detained Angel at least 12 times since 1976.

She claimed he was not detained on 2 June because the computer database was not complete and it did not list his entire previous record.

Meissner did admit undocumented immigrants were often caught up to eight times in Santa Teresa, New Mexico, where Angel had been apprehended, before they were actually prosecuted.

Meissner looked embarrassed as she answered questions at a Dallas news conference and tried to defend her agency's inability to hold on to America's most wanted man.

'Obviously, we look at a case like this, and it's horrifying that somebody like this could exist and could be at large,' Meissner said. 'My reaction was, "Did something fail here?" And I want to know, if it did, what was it and what can be done about it so it doesn't happen again.'

The fact that the mistake only came to light when the INS finally produced a photograph of Angel taken at his 2 June arrest simply compounded the error.

Other law-enforcement officials were stunned by the INS situation. Fayette County Sheriff Rick Vandel told newsmen, 'It absolutely makes me want to cry.'

Then further evidence of the INS failure to pursue Angel soon enough came to light. A Justice Department spokesman admitted to reporters that the INS had only just admitted that the West University Place Police had warned them about the alleged serial killer back in December after the slaying of Claudia Benton.

It looked as if Angel Resendez had some evil force on his side willing him on to get away with committing more killings. Luck was certainly on his side.

News of the hunt for Angel was on virtually every front page and TV news broadcast. A typical example was on Houston's Action News 5 where an anchorman told viewers, 'Despite over 1,200 calls and tips to police, Rafael Resendez-Ramirez is still one step ahead of police and leading them from state to state. Police say they are intensifying the hunt every hour.'

Each time such a statement came out in public, it knocked another nail in the task force's morale because they did not have a clue where Angel Resendez was.

On 29 June 1999, police in Las Cruces, New Mexico, fielded calls from at least four people claiming they'd seen the so-called Railway Killer in the area.

Law-enforcement officials in New Mexico had been alerted two weeks earlier to be on the lookout for him as task force officials believed Angel might visit friends in the state following his earlier imprisonment.

Meanwhile, diligent Texas Ranger Drew Carter had made further progress with Angel's sister Manuela Maturino in Albuquerque. He reported back to his superiors that he believed she was now prepared to do everything in her power to persuade her brother to surrender. Not many fellow investigators shared Drew Carter's optimism.

On that same day – 29 June – Angel Resendez was publicly linked for the first time to the 1 October 1998 bludgeoning death of an elderly woman in her rail-side home in Hughes Springs, Texas. Hughes Springs Police Chief Randy Kennedy told newsmen he was '98 per cent sure' Angel had killed 87-year-old Leafie Mason.

'The reason I'm so confident is because of the similarities in the way the crimes were committed,' Kennedy explained.

The Mason case bore striking similarities to a number of the other slayings being linked to their suspect.

1. The killer chose a random house near railway tracks.

2. He struck between midnight and dawn.
3. He used a weapon of convenience that was
   left behind.
4. He stole a small amount of cash and jewellery.

Chief Kennedy did admit that fingerprints taken at the Mason house had been lost because high humidity caused the ink to smudge. He insisted he had a set of palm prints that would back up his theory.

The only problem was that neither the FBI nor the local police had Angel's palm prints. Luck, once again, seemed to be on Angel's side.

The police chief admitted he'd have to wait until Angel was apprehended to compare the prints. 'If I get my hands on him, I'm going to body roll him in ink,' he said.

Chief Kennedy was 'chomping at the bit'. But he'd waited nine months, so he could wait another few days.

However, Kennedy's confidence that Angel would be apprehended was not shared by the FBI task force. And the fact that Angel had left a number of Satan-style markings daubed on the walls of some of his victims' homes was still not being made public in case it was crucial to the case against the Railway Killer after he was apprehended.

The FBI's command centre in Houston continued to process the thousands of leads that had poured in since Angel's details were posted on the Most Wanted list.

Authorities knew only too well that it was dangerous to focus their search on any particular region of the country as Angel was more than likely to be on the move by train or even stolen car.

Then Houston Police publicly identified 13 pieces of jewellery recovered from Angel's home in Rodeo as belonging to his alleged schoolteacher victim Noemi Dominguez. Investigators also confirmed that further forensic tests in her apartment had established Angel had definitely been present when Dominguez was murdered.

Photos of other personal items found at the house in Rodeo had already been distributed to investigators around the country.

Still in Houston, Dr Claudia Benton's husband George told investigators he recognised a pair of earrings, a necklace and a brooch also recovered from Angel and Julieta's home in Rodeo.

~

On 6 July 1999, two people, including a National Park Service ranger, reported seeing a man resembling Angel close to a New Mexico rail line near Mountainair.

It wasn't until the following day that police announced the man seen running near the railway tracks was the son of a local park ranger out jogging. Yet another false sighting of Angel Resendez could only benefit the man himself as he avoided capture.

And Don C. Clark would soon have to explain to his bosses at FBI headquarters in Washington how a Mexican drifter had managed to slip through the net of one of the biggest manhunts of the 1990s.

The bureau was coming under increasing criticism

for its handling of the operation. No longer could the INS solely take the blame following their release of Angel back on 2 June.

Many were asking why Operation Stop Train was not launched sooner. Also, if Angel had been on the FBI's Most Wanted list earlier, he might have been stopped in his tracks, they argued.

Critics wanted the answers to four vital questions.

1) Why didn't the FBI and police act faster to clarify Angel's real name so that people who actually knew him across the border would have informed on his movements more readily?

2) Why didn't the FBI rush through forensic testing to positively establish if Angel had been involved in many of the alleged killings?

3) Why weren't warning posters and public announcements made sooner about Angel Resendez and the fact he was a serial killer on the loose?

4) Why didn't investigators visit Angel's hometown of Rodeo sooner? If they had, they might have prevented a lot more bloodshed.

~

Despite a vast public response, Angel remained one step ahead of the FBI and its task force. Yet he'd been first linked to a possible killing spree six months earlier after bludgeoning Claudia Benton to death.

The Operation Stop Train task force was reduced to relying on the public to help their desperate search for the serial killer. Many members of the task force couldn't even agree about the best way to continue the investigation. Some were convinced the Railway Killer was still hopping trains because there had been no sightings of him in Mexico since he'd left Rodeo in mid-June. Other investigators believed Angel would avoid trains because he knew everyone was searching for him. They reckoned he was hiding out somewhere just inside the Mexican border.

Railway communities were still living in fear of their lives – and they were blaming the FBI for allowing this serial killer to roam the nation. Many of them described the initial FBI warnings about a supposed railway killer as 'pathetic'.

Meanwhile, Angel had become something he never wanted to be: the most famous face in America. And he wasn't even bothering to use any of the so-called elaborate disguises the FBI kept making public warnings about.

Angel Resendez's picture was plastered on magazines, newspapers and TV newscasts. But for the moment he seemed to have eluded all his pursuers.

The FBI tried to put more pressure on Angel's relatives in the US and Mexico by warning them they could be in danger because he might come after them. But that tactic had little or no effect as most of Angel's relatives insisted he would not hurt a fly.

On 8 July, the fear and panic about where suspected serial killer Angel might next strike was so great that the son-in-law of the Mayor of Artesia, California, found himself arrested just because his name was Ramirez and he vaguely resembled Angel, along with tens of thousands of others.

The cold harsh truth was that investigators believed that the best chance of capturing Angel would be if he came out of hiding and killed again.

24.

To the American public, the Railway Killer was a twisted psycho who thrived on the thrill of the quick kill. He was portrayed as a control freak who fully understood the limitations of his acts of violence. Many believed that he enjoyed leaving evidence of his crimes to taunt investigators.

One criminologist, University of Louisville professor Ronald M Holmes, insisted, 'This is a power-seeking endeavour. It's an aphrodisiac. It makes him feel good.'

Holmes had profiled more than 375 murder and rape cases for police departments across the country and written several books on serial killers. He believed that Angel's motives were straight out of the serial killer textbook.

Basically there are four different types of serial killers.
1. The visionary type hears voices ordering him to commit violent acts.

2. The mission type kills anyone he or she perceives as 'undesirable', typically prostitutes or the homeless.

3. The hedonistic type kills to get some sort of sexual thrill from the act itself.

4. The power control type, who kills because the act of murder gives him a sense of omnipotence.

Expert Ronald Holmes labelled the Railway Killer as a Number-4 type. 'That seems to be him. There doesn't seem to be anything overtly sexual about all the attacks.

'There's a lot of risk in beating people to death, and it takes a lot of energy. If they're hit from the front, if he can see the face of the person he's terrorising, that gives him more of a high, makes him feel strong and invincible.'

Amazingly, psychologist Holmes was referring to a man often seen in his hometown gently cycling around the dusty streets with his pet dog running alongside him.

But understanding the Railway Killer's true motivation in bludgeoning and shooting at least eight people to death was perplexing to say the least. He picked his victims at random. But some investigators believed that his pattern made sense to him, if to no one else.

Ronald Holmes insisted that, because of his small physical size, the Railway Killer had to be very careful about who he picked on. 'He has to rely on a blitz attack and people he can control,' he explained.

Investigators were further confused when the

Railway Killer changed his method of killing by shooting George Morber. They presumed that Morber had tried to physically challenge his attacker who then panicked and grabbed Morber's gun and fired.

Investigators knew that, as serial killers move on, they start to kill differently. There was a bizarre learning process that went with such criminal territory.

Holmes explained, 'All the serial killers I've talked to describe this overwhelming compulsion to kill – and where that comes from exactly I don't know. It's probably with them from birth. But the more they kill, the better they get at it, and the more economical they get.'

Most experts were convinced that Angel Resendez was deliberately leaving his fingerprints behind at the scene of every crime.

Holmes explained, 'He's not so dumb. It's a form of advertisement. It's to let you know, "I'm still here." He doesn't want to get caught. Picture the most pleasurable thing you like to do – would you want to stop?'

Tom Vingar of the Texas Department of Public Safety agreed with Ronald Holmes's assessment. 'This guy is just totally sadistic,' said Vingar. 'He's deliberately selecting people like some kind of animal.' And in the back of all the investigators' minds was the fear that there were other victims out there that no one yet knew about. Vingar pointed out, 'Ted Bundy started killing when he was fifteen-and-a-half. Think about it.'

Vingar and other investigators feared that 400 task

force officers based in Houston alone would do little to prevent more bloodshed before Angel was apprehended.

He didn't have to kill these people. But he was *choosing* to – and there was no indication he'd stop killing. He'd proven he could literally be anywhere any time. He knew that the task force was on his trail, but it didn't seem to bother him.

Many believed that the alleged rail-riding serial killer Angel was exploiting an ability to 'shift back and forth between cultures' to hamper the nationwide manhunt.

Lexington-based forensic psychiatrist Dr Robert Granacher, Jr warned that bilingual Angel had 'the opportunity to hide in ways many criminals wouldn't be able to manage'.

The hopes of an early capture still looked unrealistic. Behind the scenes, Angel's relatives in California, Texas, New Mexico and Mexico were co-operative with FBI and Texas Ranger investigators. But agents admitted privately that interviews with them had not uncovered 'anything earth shattering' about Angel Resendez.

Many investigators felt this line of enquiry was not worthwhile. As Tom Vingar insisted, 'This guy is very detached from his family circles. That's what makes him so difficult to find. It's a different ballgame from most people you encounter.

'He's not checking in along the way. He's used to travelling without human comforts. He hangs out in places where he can blend in.'

Texas Ranger Drew Carter did not agree with this

appraisal and he continued to try and keep in constant contact with certain members of Angel Resendez's family, especially his sister in Albuquerque.

Ultimately, the task force still had no real idea why Angel had gone on such an orgy of violence and destruction.

Vingar added, 'We don't know why he turned so violent or if it's a recent thing or if there are other victims we don't know about. It's a complete mystery.'

Meanwhile, one of the biggest manhunts in US criminal history continued. But most of the Operation Stop Train team believed that the Railway Killer would only be caught through some kind of luck or accident, not solid police work.

~

Angel's ability to disappear into thin air once he had committed a slaying was not the only thing baffling Operation Stop Train investigators. They couldn't understand why no one had a bad word to say about him south of the border.

Angel's uncle Rafael Resendez-Ramirez had more reason than most to be angry at his nephew because Angel had regularly used his name during his travels. The result was that the FBI had labelled 'Rafael Resendez-Ramirez' as the most wanted man in North America.

Resendez-Ramirez insisted to Mexican and US investigators that the man he knew as 'Angel' was not capable of the crimes he was being linked with. Also, he complained bitterly to FBI agents about the way his name had been linked to Angel.

'His real name is Angel Reyes Resendez. Please can you stop telling everyone my name. I am becoming famous because of him. I have not killed anyone,' he told a group of investigators who visited him at his home in San Nicholas Tolentino, a tiny farming village 65 miles southeast of Mexico City.

He even passed on a message to his nephew through the FBI, 'Angel, if you have committed these errors, I beg you to confront them as men should.'

But Resendez-Ramirez told agents he doubted that his nephew had committed the crimes, telling investigators that all the evidence they had mentioned sounded like 'speculation'.

'So who is the witness?' he asked one bemused agent.

~

In Albuquerque, Texas Ranger Drew Carter paid yet another visit to Angel Resendez's sister Manuela. He was by now convinced that the suspected Railway Killer was in touch with her.

Carter told colleagues Manuela was now even more convinced her brother might be guilty of the killings and she would eventually be the key to his capture.

Many of the task force members back in Houston remained sceptical about using Angel's family to try to broker a surrender. But there didn't seem any harm in allowing one young Ranger to continue getting alongside the family.

In Ciudad Juarez, alleged serial killer Angel was then officially linked with up to 15 homicides throughout the Mexican state of Chihuahua.

Steve Slater, an adviser to the Chihuahua State Public Safety Department, told reporters, 'We are looking at homicides we haven't cleared that appear to fit this method. There are some that are unsolved that may fit him.'

At least eight of the alleged murders in Juarez had elements in common with the eight slayings the Railway Killer had so far been directly linked to. Investigators knew that Angel still had relatives, including his own mother, living in Juarez.

Slater said, 'He's been through here a lot. We certainly have railway tracks and bodies found by railway tracks, and most are women.'

If Angel was implicated in these Mexican killings, it would be doubly ironic that the INS had sent him back to Ciudad Juarez when they failed to recognise him as a wanted homicide suspect back on 2 June.

~

Having nudged aside the notorious terrorist Osama bin Laden as Public Enemy Number One after his elevation to the top of the FBI's Most Wanted List, soft-spoken Angel Resendez was now the ultimate figure of fear to Middle America.

Handgun shops in areas where he'd allegedly killed reported a sharp increase in the sale of weapons. That once friendly shriek of a freight train had become a sound which prompted fear and trepidation among many hundreds of thousands of Americans.

The entire nation was aware that a homicidal hobo was riding the rails, killing his victims completely at random, and no one could even find him.

In early July, further details of Angel's methods were publicly disclosed by authorities for the first time. Investigators revealed that his trademark was to pound in his victim's skull with a sledgehammer or heavy rock. Then on some occasions he would cover their head with a blanket. Then he'd toy with the body while he sat and watched his victim die.

It was also revealed publicly for the first time that Angel did not just hurry off into the night after committing his dreadful deed. There was clear evidence that he sometimes lingered long enough to raid the fridge and rifle through the drawers of his victims' homes.

These actions were interpreted as the 'calling card' of a homicidal maniac.

25

FBI task force chief Don C. Clark was astounded by the number of police departments across the nation contacting him about Angel's possible connection to numerous unsolved killings.

'Comparisons are going on as we speak,' Clark told a press conference in Houston.

The last time anyone could remember so many cases being linked to one killer was when drifter Henry Lee Lucas became the chief suspect in more than 600 slayings across America. The beginning of the end for Lucas came on 16 September 1982, with the discovery of the body of Kate Pearl Rich of Ringgold, Texas. A few months before she died, Lucas and his 'common-law wife', 15-year-old Frieda Powell, had helped Rich around the house in exchange for room and board.

Following his incarceration for that murder, Lucas claimed he'd murdered hundreds of others. But, given his cavalier disregard for the truth, most of these claims were later discounted. But he did definitely stab his mother to death and had served 15 years of a 24-year sentence before he was released from jail only to kill again.

Meanwhile, Operation Stop Train leader Clark and his investigators knew that they had to tread carefully in regard to all these other possible cases because there was no immediate way to establish how many were really connected to Angel Resendez.

Jim Mattox, a former Texas attorney general and outspoken critic of the Henry Lee Lucas investigation, warned that police should not try to pin any of these other killings on Angel until after the current cases were brought to justice.

Agent Clark insisted this would not happen.

~

Whoever telephoned Angel Resendez and warned him to get out of Rodeo definitely instilled in the suspected Railway Killer a genuine fear that bounty hunters were about to come over the border and grab him for the $125,000 reward money on offer.

And Angel knew that such characters were just as likely to shoot first and ask questions later. Professional bail agents across the United States are, on the whole, responsible, law-abiding citizens with a code of ethics was supposed to prevent the very shootings that Angel was so fearful about.

But virtually every week there was at least one

incident that suggested a trigger-happy minority could cause great harm to the bounty hunters' cause.

And those were the people whom Angel Resendez truly feared.

Then, yet another alleged sighting of Angel Resendez – still referred to in the media as Rafael Resendez-Ramirez – was made at a bar in his old stamping ground of Mountainair, in New Mexico.

Local county undersheriff Don Packingham insisted to reporters that he and his deputies had been just a few minutes from apprehending America's most wanted man. He explained, 'A guy matching his description had stopped for a beer in Mountainair. We picked up the glass and are checking it for prints.'

Not surprisingly, Undersheriff Packingham presumed he had taken a train south out of Mountainair. Results of the fingerprints taken at the scene later showed he was not their man.

On 8 July, frustrated federal investigators showed just how worried they really were about the fugitive Railway Killer by making a public appeal to him to 'do the right thing and give himself up'.

It was a desperate measure. Despite thousands of leads and dozens of reported sightings of the man they still called 'Rafael Resendez-Ramirez' he had successfully eluded some of the nation's finest detectives.

The FBI and INS – still embarrassed at how they let him slip through their hands – reminded the public about the $125,000 reward still on offer for information leading to the capture of Angel. The INS pointed out that anyone with information – even undocumented immigrants – could qualify for the reward.

Richard Cravener, INS district director in Houston, insisted there were ways to provide temporary visas to those who agreed to co-operate with the investigation.

He added, 'Anyone with information to assist in the apprehension of Rafael Resendez-Ramirez should come forward.'

FBI task force chief Don C. Clark admitted publicly for the first time that his agents had been in touch with Angel's common-law wife Julieta and insisted 'she wants him to turn himself in to authorities'.

He added, 'I would also like to plead with Mr Ramirez that he should turn himself in.' Even the top FBI man continued to use Angel's incorrect name.

The only matter that FBI special agent Clark seemed reluctant to be drawn on was whether Julieta had travelled to the United States to help investigators. However, Clark did make a point of saying that he had personally assured her that his agents were not out to harm Angel, only to bring him to justice.

What Clark didn't mention was that Texas Ranger Drew Carter had by this stage formed such a close bond with Angel's sister in Albuquerque that he was now predicting that it was only a matter of days before he could persuade the most wanted man in the nation to surrender peacefully.

The FBI remained sceptical that such an event would ever happen.

~

There was much that was still deeply mysterious and contradictory about Angel Resendez as the early days of July 1999 found the vast Operation Train Stop task force no nearer to locating America's most wanted man.

Investigators had labelled him a spree killer because of the nature of his crimes, but that had not made it any easier to find him. In fact, in some ways it was an admission that this was going to be a long, gruelling operation.

As FBI spokesman Mike Fabregas explained, 'Wherever he decides to stop, he stops. He has no connection whatsoever with his victims. They are just in the wrong place at the wrong time.'

Angel tended to use any weapon which was handy. Sometimes he sexually assaulted his victims; sometimes not. Sometimes he stole; sometimes not. This lack of consistency really was an investigator's nightmare.

Some of the task force members privately conceded that they had a sneaking respect for Angel because he was so resourceful. He had countless documents to support his many assumed names. And they believed he was changing his appearance constantly.

But the fact remained that, even though he had spent 11 of the previous 20 years in jails in California, Texas, Florida and New Mexico, investigators could not provide a definitive description of their fugitive.

And the most important point of all was: How did an unassuming petty criminal turn into a mass murderer?

Operation Stop Train investigators even went back through Angel Resendez's prison files. In Florida –

where he spent his longest sentence – State Corrections spokeswoman Debbie Buchanan told the task force, 'There's nothing in the file that would distinguish him from any other inmate. It's almost as if he woke up one day and snapped.'

Then there was the ever-deepening mystery of those markings the Railway Killer left at many of the murder sites.

Investigators were so baffled by these markings that they had yet to conclude what they really meant. And they were still keeping their existence a secret in case it created problems with copycats or evidence once they had detained their chief suspect.

And then there was the nation's ongoing fascination – some would even call it an obsession – with serial killers.

Angel seemed to personify a fear of mayhem coming up from south of the border, bringing terror and death. His victims were white and respectable, not prostitutes or drifters.

He had truly become a criminal enigma.

The FBI's Operation Stop Train was supposed to be enveloping every corner of the nation, but it had so far failed to even find a trace of a slight, poorly educated Mexican drifter with a propensity for drugs, alcohol and murder.

~

Just over a century ago, the first homicide to be solved by a fingerprint happened in Argentina. In a small town near Buenos Aires, two children were found bludgeoned to death.

The mother pointed the finger of accusation against a young peasant who she said was in love with her; she said he had threatened to murder her and her children.

The peasant agreed that he had threatened her but said he had not meant it. He stuck to his story, despite intense interrogation from local police. He also just happened to mention that he was jealous of the woman's lover – a man who refused to marry her because of her 'illegitimate brats'.

When a detective in charge of the case found a bloodstained fingerprint on the door of the woman's bedroom, he remembered reading that every fingerprint was unique.

He had the door removed and brought to his office. Then he took the woman's fingerprints with an ink pad. A magnifying glass revealed that the bloodstained print was that of her right thumb. She quickly confessed that she had killed her children so her lover would marry her.

The Argentine government was so impressed with fingerprinting that it decided to set up a general register of identification that would involve fingerprinting everyone in the country. But there was an outcry, and the idea was abandoned.

In the last decade, some police forces across the US have taken a courageous step in response to a recent surge in the most heinous crime of all – murder.

For they have been taking not only fingerprints and photographs whenever they arrest a suspect, but also a mouth swab which contains a sample of DNA, the molecule that is also a unique genetic fingerprint of every individual.

This information is matched against the file of all unsolved crimes across most of the nation. The result has been a rise in detection figures. But the forces who have adopted this scheme have a problem – the same problem encountered in Argentina more than a century ago.

For taking DNA is still in some states seen as a violation of civil rights – even though samples from suspects who are not charged are immediately destroyed.

At the beginning of this century, the US had a far lower crime rate than it does today.

Communities like Gorham, Illinois and Weimar, Texas, were then sleepy backwaters where no one locked their houses or cars. But now, thanks to the Railway Killer, this was no longer the case.

Yet many lives could have been saved and Angel Resendez's murderous reign brought to a speedier end if that nationwide computer system had been fully operational. In other words, he might well have been stopped before he turned into a serial killer. Angel had been in prison numerous times so all the DNA was available. But the state of Kentucky was not part of the patchy nationwide DNA computer network.

Sooner or later, police across the entire US are going to have to fully co-operate with each other and be prepared to routinely administer DNA test.

With a properly run national database, it is plausible that Angel Resendez would never have become

America's most wanted man – a serial killer who could go down in its grisly criminal history.

~

On 8 July 1999, the legislator who authored a 1992 law creating Kentucky's database of crime-related DNA samples sparked a storm of controversy by asking why, nine months after the FBI's national DNA database went online, Kentucky still was not a participant.

'Our DNA database was not intended to sit on the shelf, but to be made immediately available once the national DNA indexing system was online,' Representative Steve Riggs, Louisville, wrote in a letter to State Police Commissioner Gary Rose, whose crime lab was supposed to be responsible for collecting and storing such samples.

The following day, the father of Lexington murder victim Christopher Maier added fuel to the fire of controversy by publicly asking whether the case could have been solved much sooner if the database had been in operation.

He was understandably concerned to hear that, even though many states had been using genetic evidence derived from DNA samples as a crime-fighting tool since the early 1990s, the FBI computer index of DNA had gone online only nine months earlier and Kentucky had still not become a participant.

26

Sunday, 11 July 1999 was a rare day off for Texas Ranger Drew Carter. His virtually round-the-clock work with Angel's family had been a draining experience over the previous few weeks. So he drove down to the Gulf Coast to enjoy a day's fishing with some boyhood friends.

He'd only just set up his rods when Angel's sister Manuela Maturino called Carter on his mobile phone from Albuquerque. 'I need to meet with you today,' she told Carter.

He knew from the tone of her voice it was important.

'I've spoken to one of Angel's friends and I think he's going to give himself up.'

Within hours, Carter, an FBI agent and a deputy US marshal were on a plane heading for Manuela's home in Albuquerque.

Virtually as soon as Carter walked into Manuela's

tiny, single-storey home, she told him, 'He wants to surrender. But he wants some assurances.'

It then emerged that the respectable, family-loving side of Angel had responded to appeals from his sister, who had told Angel it was a matter of honour.

Manuela had come to like and trust Drew Carter throughout the long days and nights of their many meetings over the previous few weeks. Carter had built up a feeling of trust between them and now it seemed to be about to pay off.

By the middle of the following day, Monday, 12 July, Drew Carter had struck a deal in which Angel, through his sister, had agreed to surrender *only* to Drew Carter himself. The Ranger gave assurances to Angel that he would only initially be charged in Texas with the burglary of victim Claudia Benton's home the previous December.

Carter also promised Angel's family that he would be given complete protection, humane treatment, a psychological evaluation and visits from family members.

That afternoon Carter asked Harris County District Attorney John Holmes to fax him an agreement to all of Angel's sister's initial demands.

Manuela Maturino then passed the offer on to a relative in Mexico.

That evening, she rang Carter to confirm that her brother would be surrendering the following day. Even Drew Carter couldn't quite believe the most wanted man in America was really about to make a peaceful surrender.

27

The remote Yselta Bridge over the Rio Grande connects Zaragosa, Mexico, with El Paso. It was the type of border crossing Angel Resendez had tried his hardest to avoid over the previous 24 years. It was far too exposed for his liking.

But on the morning of 13 July 1999, the grit-filled breeze whistled around Angel's ankles as he began walking slowly and deliberately along the empty pedestrian sidewalk arched with mesh fencing to stop anyone from jumping down to the often bone-dry riverbed below.

An eerie silence enveloped the entire scene. Shuffling in his customary manner, but steadily and without hesitation, Angel looked up into the scorching sunlight grid and glanced at the gathering of mainly uniformed figures standing just 100 yards ahead. Angel stopped for a split second and then continued what must have been the longest three-minute walk of his entire life.

He was about to surrender to the authorities of the most powerful nation on earth. In his leather work boots, striped grey cotton shirt and dark jeans, he didn't exactly fit most people's perception of a blood-hungry serial killer who viciously bludgeoned innocent people to death.

On the US side of the bridge, Texas Ranger Drew Carter turned slowly to one of his colleagues standing at the border checkpoint and said simply, 'This is going to happen.'

Carter had immediately recognised Angel. As he later explained, 'That's a face that has just been shown all over the country for a long period of time now, and it's a face that I've been working on. So, when I did see that face, there was a little bit of excitement there.'

Angel was fulfilling the agreement brokered by his sister because, as the people of Rodeo always insisted, he was a man of his word.

Just behind him as he continued that lonely walk across the bridge were his brother, sister and a pastor. They had all been given special leave by the INS to walk across the bridge. Despite the enormity of what he was doing, Angel remained calm and utterly unprepossessing.

When he finally reached the crossing line between Mexico and the US, he looked up at tall, young Texas Ranger Drew Carter complete with his white Stetson and extended his hand. This was the man his sister had said he could trust with his life. Carter, waiting with two other officers, shook Angel's hand warmly, almost as if he was greeting a long-lost friend. Then, almost apologetically, he clipped a pair of handcuffs around Angel's wrists and pointed the way to a waiting white Texas Ranger sedan.

Angel Resendez's short walk across that bridge on 13 July meant he was voluntarily leaving a country with no death penalty and entering a state with the most executions per year in the United States.

And, throughout the task force, there was a sneaking admiration for the personal rapport nurtured between Texas Ranger Drew Carter and Angel's sister in Albuquerque.

~

Less than two hours after that fateful walk across the bridge, Angel Resendez stood shackled before a Texas criminal law magistrate in El Paso. He listened silently to a burglary charge against him.

When asked if he had any questions, he murmured, 'No, sir,' in a soft voice that showed little hint of emotion, although it was far from cold.

Outside the court, law-enforcement officials could only shake their heads and wonder why it had all ended so peacefully.

'I'm not absolutely sure of the reason why he surrendered,' said Captain Bruce Casteel. 'I've been in this business a very long time and I'm struggling to answer that myself.'

On that same afternoon, a beaming Don C. Clark insisted to a press conference of hundreds of journalists that the driving pressure of hundreds of law officers and '200 million eyes' nationwide as well as bounty hunters on both sides of the border ultimately convinced Angel he had no place to hide.

There was no word yet on whether the $125,000 reward would go to members of Angel's family.

And Clark was not as open with his gratitude towards Ranger Drew Carter as some hoped he might be. When asked if any single law-enforcement agency had led the way in the capture of the most dangerous man in North America, Clark replied, 'No.'

Behind him stood Ranger Drew Carter. He raised his eyebrows as the FBI chief answered, before a broad smile came to his lips.

However, behind the scenes, Texas authorities were angered by Clark's complete failure to acknowledge Carter's sterling work in bringing the fugitive to justice. They were particularly annoyed that the FBI decided to circumvent the Rangers by almost instantly announcing the arrest in Washington.

Clark compounded that irritation even further by telling the press conference, 'The investigation left Resendez with no place to turn. The pressure finally got to him.'

The FBI also revealed that police authorities across the US were anxious to speak to Angel Resendez about approximately 70 other unsolved murders that resembled his MO.

Clark said, 'Texas has him first but there are a lot of other states that want to interview Resendez. This is only just the beginning of a long legal process that may well involve many other homicides.'

It was only after the FBI press conference that Drew Carter was asked about his efforts to get the alleged serial killer to surrender. 'Honesty's never hard. Sincerity is something people sense. That's what I did. I was honest with the family.'

~

After his brief court appearance, Angel Resendez was flown to Houston on an FBI-supplied Lear jet.

From there he was escorted by half a dozen Texas Rangers to the Houston Police Department, where he was questioned and underwent DNA testing at a city crime lab. Officials insisted that he had not requested an attorney and that he was fully co-operating with detectives.

At that stage, Angel had only been charged with murder outside Texas – in Kentucky and Illinois – as well as the burglary charge in Texas. This had been one of the conditions Drew Carter had promised during negotiations for his surrender. In Harris County, prosecutors said they planned to upgrade that burglary charge to capital murder once they got back the results of the DNA testing the following week.

Then Angel Resendez was driven in a ten-vehicle convoy to the Harris County Jail, while the FBI continued to sift through numerous requests from law-enforcement agencies across the nation who believed he might have committed unlawful killings in their jurisdiction.

Adjusting to life in a 60-ft-sq cell among 8,300 inmates was hardly something knew to Angel, but he was relieved to find himself being kept in solitary confinement.

The authorities had also put him under a 24-hour suicide watch, which also suited Angel because it meant he was never entirely alone.

'Because of the high profile of the case, he's under administrative segregation,' explained spokeswoman Celeste Spaugh. 'A deputy has constant visual observation of him.'

Angel's cell was pretty standard – a bed, sink and toilet. But he was told he would be allowed one hour's recreation time on the prison roof every day. Angel told staff he was most concerned that two officers should accompany him at all times.

As one investigator explained, 'He was still freaked out that everyone was trying to kill him to get at that reward. The guy trusted no one.'

And some of Angel's fears were not completely without foundation. Some of the other prisoners at Harris County would dearly have loved to get at their 'celebrity inmate' just to create a bit of attention.

The only time the suspected Railway Killer showed a glimpse of a bad temper was when officials confiscated his Bible after insisting that jail rules did not allow inmates to bring anything into the jail. 'He can always buy one in the commissary for five dollars,' said jail spokeswoman Celeste Spaugh.

The jail also refused Angel's request for kosher food because it was not based on health or religions reasons. Angel had not helped his case by insisting to enforcement agents after his initial arrest that he was 'Jewish, Christian, all religions'.

As Spaugh explained, 'We don't place much stock in his request. He'll have to do a better job proving it.'

In Englewood, Colorado, minister Mark Sirnic, brother of one of Angel's alleged victim, the Reverend Norman 'Skip' Sirnic, voiced tempered satisfaction that the fugitive had finally been apprehended. 'It has been my prayer that he would be apprehended before he hurt anyone else. That prayer has been answered. I don't have any vengeful feelings, a vendetta that he be put to death.

'My main hope is that he is kept off the streets. But it's a consequence in Texas for the crimes that were committed. If you're going to commit a crime, you'd better be willing to deal with the consequences.'

Various experts were soon lining up to explain their interpretation of Angel's decision to surrender. 'Really, by walking over the bridge to turn himself in... he probably just sacrificed his life,' said Sandra Guars, a criminal law professor at the University of Houston.

~

Angel Resendez was in a talkative mood in the hours following his surrender – about anything except the nine slayings he was suspected of having committed. He gabbed into the wee small hours of that dramatic Tuesday, telling detectives his opinions about US foreign policy, economics and mathematics.

One of those present was Sergeant Tom Ladd. He noticed how Angel would either turn the conversation back to what he wanted to talk about or he would simply not answer the questions being put to him about his crimes.

Angel yapped on about his displeasure with capitalism, the treatment of migrant workers and numerous US government policies, including the recent air campaign in Yugoslavia. And he made it crystal clear he did not like America or Americans.

'If you don't like this country,' asked Ladd, 'why d'you always come here?'

Angel looked across at his interrogator and stared softly into his eyes with a blank stare, but he did not reply.

Moments later, he switched back to discussing a mathematical theory concerning the numeral zero. 'You got a pen and paper?' Angel asked Ladd.

The officer got it for him immediately, hopeful that this might suddenly be a turning point in the interrogation process.

'Thanks,' said Angel as he took the pen and paper. Then he proceeded to sketch a formula he claimed would solve the mathematical problem.

From the moment of his surrender, Angel had happily agreed to speak to investigators without an attorney present. But all those who encountered him noticed how careful he was not to admit or deny his part in any crime.

Ladd noted that Angel's demeanour throughout his initial interrogation was the same meek, soft-spoken persona he had shown in the courtroom. The officer dismissed any notions that Angel was not of sound mind or that he had been hoodwinked into surrendering with a possible death sentence looming.

'His mental capacity was just fine,' Ladd later recalled.

Within hours of Angel's capture, President Bill Clinton joined the bandwagon of congratulations for law-enforcement officials.

Interrupting a day-long visit to Miami Beach, Florida, he told reporters, 'All Americans can rest easier. I want to thank all of the state, local and federal law-enforcement officials whose hard work led to the surrender of the suspected "Railway Killer" earlier today.'

The President then added, 'As a result of their determined efforts and the co-operation of Mexican authorities, the suspect is now in custody in the United States. We now know that law-enforcement authorities will bring the full force of the law to bear in this case.'

The back-slapping continued in the hours after Angel surrendered when FBI Director Louis J Freeh issued a statement to commemorate the capture of the country's most wanted fugitive.

He tactfully cited the FBI's 'gratitude' to the special law-enforcement task force in Houston and 'many other law-enforcement agencies whose relentless search led today to the arrest of Rafael Resendez-Ramirez, one of the most dangerous accused offenders placed on the FBI's list of Ten Most Wanted Fugitives in recent years'.

Freeh continued, 'Scores of law-enforcement agencies were greatly aided by railway police, the Immigration and Naturalization Service, and a host of other organisations and individuals in being able to deny the defendant safe haven or places to hide.'

Freeh even praised the media. 'The news media deserves enormous credit for genuine public service in its coverage of the search for Resendez-Ramirez, coverage that made a significant contribution to the successful conclusion to the huge manhunt.'

In Texas, it was duly noted that there had been no specific mention of the Rangers, but then they had become used to such oversights by the FBI.

As one local enforcement agent commented, 'The fact that Freeh praised the INS sums up just how meaningless his statement was. It was nothing more than a diplomatic slap on the FBI's back. A disgrace.'

But, if the FBI thought they'd heard the last of Ranger Drew Carter's single-handed effort to capture the nation's most wanted man, they were in for a big surprise.

Within two days of Angel's surrender, the fuss over who should get the full credit for the fugitive's surrender was fascinating the nation in the light of the highly publicised end to the manhunt.

There was just no getting away from the fact that by all accounts – other than those of Don C. Clark – the remarkable surrender was orchestrated by Texas Ranger Drew Carter.

The Rangers' parent agency, the Department of Public Safety in Texas, even tersely announced that they had been preparing to announce Angel's capture when the FBI stepped in and beat them to it.

Spokesman Mike Cox explained, 'But we had not done so yet because we here at the Austin headquarters had not received word yet that Resendez was taken into custody. Suddenly, we began getting calls from media hearing that Resendez was taken into custody.'

Cox added tactfully, 'The FBI has tremendous resources and has helped us over the years.'

Drew Carter's boss, Ranger Captain Earl Pearson, also tried to diplomatically play down the situation. But everyone inside the task force knew that it was Carter's excellent field work in establishing such a good rapport with Angel's sister in Albuquerque that had been crucial to getting her brother to surrender.

Ranger Carter refused to take sole credit for Angel Resendez's capture, but it was clear to all the other enforcement agencies involved in the hunt for the fugitive that Carter had pulled it off virtually single-handedly.

As Mike Cox explained, 'This really, as far as we can tell, would not have happened without Ranger Carter.'

Then Carter was allowed to explain the full extent of his role and why the family co-operated. 'They love their brother and their relative and they care for him deeply, but at the same time they had been co-operative in this investigation and were doing what they felt was the right thing.

'There were very personal, one-on-one discussions with family members representing the subject and myself and other people that brought this about,' Carter said. 'Honesty's never hard. Sincerity is something people sense... that's what I did. I was honest with the whole family.'

He also explained, 'I think it's a big relief to everybody involved: the law-enforcement officers that are working the case, the victims' families, as well, and I suspect the fugitive himself and his family.'

But many of the investigators involved in the manhunt believed there was a lot more at stake in Angel's surrender than just the reputation of a young Ranger.

They believed that Angel surrendered because of the Rangers' impeccable reputation. 'Their word is their bond,' explained San Antonio defence lawyer Jesse Gamas, whose mainly Latin clientele hail from both sides of the border.

'I think what Resendez was scared of was bounty hunters, or people taking potshots at him, or people bringing him out of Mexico with no guarantee. I think he trusted the Rangers enough to cut a deal with them because they would keep their word with him.'

Meanwhile, special agent Clark continued to try and play it all down by insisting the FBI was not trying to steal the spotlight from the Rangers and their parent organisation the DPS.

However, many inside both Texas law-enforcement agencies still recalled that it was the FBI – not the DPS – that had mounted the assault on the Branch Davidian compound near Waco in 1993 after a bungled Bureau of Alcohol, Tobacco and Firearms raid resulted in a deadly shoot-out and a 51-day standoff.

The FBI siege had ended with a fire that destroyed the compound and left cult leader David Koresh and about 80 followers dead.

~

The first clue as to how Angel Resendez might try to use his Mexican nationality to avoid the death penalty was made by his court-appointed lawyer Allen Tanner.

'We hope the Mexican consulate here can bring some pressure upon authorities not to seek the death penalty,' he said.

The trial of Angel Resendez was going to be a far from cut-and-dried affair.

In the little community of Weimar so brutally torn apart by the violent deaths of the Reverend Sirnic and his wife and Josephine Konvicka, a new preacher had taken over at the United Church. Reverend Ralph Ludwig said, 'We're hoping that everybody can start sleeping again, because there have been a lot of people who were not sleeping well.'

But life would never be quite the same in Weimar.

28

On 14 July – the day after his surrender on that bridge in El Paso – the man law-enforcement agents across the nation had named as 'Rafael Resendez-Ramirez' told a Texas district court judge in Houston that his real name was Angel Maturino Resendez.

Yet, despite being arraigned under that name on burglary charges, not one official in court that morning was certain if he was telling the truth.

Only three weeks earlier, the FBI had held a dramatic press conference to announce that the man they considered to be Public Enemy Number One had a completely different name from the one he was now using. Even nailing down Angel's name was proving tricky.

The fact of the matter was that Angel Resendez had successfully confused US authorities for more than 20 years with his ever-changing identity.

Police, border officials, judges and prosecutors had all struggled to get a handle on his name – along with some very basic information since he first tried to enter the US illegally back in 1976.

All they did know for certain was that, since his first brush with the border patrol, Angel had collected a mountain of identification cards – including voter registration cards, birth certificates and even library cards.

Angel had even used one alias – Jose Konig Mengele – as a twisted 'tribute' to one of his alleged heroes, Nazi concentration camp doctor Josef Mengele.

Meanwhile, attorneys who had prosecuted Angel in the past said that, while it was not uncommon for criminals to use one or two aliases, they were baffled as to why Angel would use dozens of names. One prosecutor said, 'Homeless drifters do not have all these cards. They're not savvy enough. We thought he might be connected to a white-collar crime ring or paramilitary group.'

While Angel's interest in fascism has already been touched upon, there is absolutely no evidence that he was in league with others.

In the days following Angel's surrender, not even Ranger Carter could get his man to say anything of any great relevance to the charges he faced.

Carter explained, 'Just because someone talks doesn't mean they are being co-operative. He has given no information pertinent to his criminal case.'

Despite his peaceful responses, Angel Resendez was

showing no signs of the remorse that Ranger Carter had suggested was behind his decision. It was starting to seem that the gentle-looking, quietly spoken ex-motor mechanic was a lot more cunning than his old friends and family back in Rodeo would ever have suspected.

Reports that the family had done a deal to get Angel off their hands and claim the $125,000 reward money were gaining momentum.

It was also rumoured that some of Rodeo's more successful criminals had 'suggested' to Angel's family and friends that he should give himself up because they were fed up with the American lawmen and journalists swarming all over their home territory.

Back in Houston, Angel remained incarcerated at the Harris County Jail and local prosecutors believed they had an airtight case.

Angel was soon inundated with offers from Houston attorneys to represent him. His chosen lawyer, Allen Tanner, immediately indicated that the rage with which Angel used to allegedly kill his victims would feature in his defence as it seemed likely he would plead insanity. Tanner was even putting it about that he wasn't sure his client had actually committed any of the murders.

But FBI officials were quick to point out that Angel was far from unintelligent and they had evidence of some of the letters he wrote while he was serving time for various criminal offences in the past.

FBI profiler Alan Brantley was one of the first criminal experts to interrogate Angel, whom he found to show clear signs of superior intelligence. 'He's an injustice collector,' said Brantley.

Detective Ken Macha also spoke to Angel soon after his arrest and concluded that he was 'politically astute'. During a one-hour interrogation, Macha also noticed that Angel implied he had a good reason for his actions. But when Macha pressed him for further details 'he would just start rambling'.

Investigators already knew that Angel had played an active role in the US Libertarian Party during the 1980s through the prison correspondence they managed to trace.

A few days after Angel's surrender, his stepbrother Florentino Maturino Resendez complained that US authorities had lied to the family about the possibility of him getting the death penalty. Resendez insisted Angel had been promised immunity from the death penalty during negotiations for his surrender.

Resendez claimed the family would not have helped convince Angel to give himself up if they had known he faced execution.

Not surprisingly, Texas state officials immediately denied the claim. 'No promises were made whatsoever,' said Tom Vingar, spokesman for the Texas Department of Public Safety, who even went so far as to emphasise the Texans' liberal use of the death penalty and how well known it was throughout the US and in Mexico. 'The person we talked to was his sister, and she understood the death penalty was a possibility.'

But Angel's lawyer Allen Tanner stepped up

the pressure by telling reporters, 'What he thinks of as humane treatment and what his family thinks of as humane treatment was Texas not seeking the death penalty.'

Vingar hit back by stating, 'It's no secret Texas has the death penalty, and it's no secret in Mexico.'

~

On the Thursday following his capture, Angel made a brief court appearance during which he was advised of his right to contact the Mexican consulate for assistance. Texas had been particularly careful to offer this, having recently been heavily criticised for failing to honour this obligation in the case of Stanley Faulder, a Canadian executed the previous month.

Later that same day, Angel received his first promised visit from his common-law wife Julieta and sister Manuela at the Harris County Jail. And that night they were each flown back to their homes in Rodeo and Albuquerque.

Meanwhile, two Texas Rangers were assigned the task of interrogating Angel. They soon concluded that, despite his pleasant demeanour, he was still being 'generally unco-operative'. Spokesman Vingar explained, 'He was talkative, but not forthcoming in regards to information tied to the cases.'

And the amount of enquiries from other police forces across the nation trying to link Angel to their unsolved murders topped 700 by the end of that first week of his detention.

There were certain disturbing elements to the Resendez family's claims about Angel not fully appreciating he was walking right into the death penalty by agreeing to surrender in Texas. The clear implication was that neither Julieta nor Angel's sister would have urged him to surrender if they had known he could die.

Ranger Drew Carter denied the claim, while other officials pointed out a strange irony. Angel's sister and brother stood to get a share of that $125,000 reward money – enough to buy him a good legal defence.

Back at the FBI's field office in Houston, investigators were still frantically analysing data and interviewing police to try to establish connections between Angel and other unsolved murder cases. So far, the Texas Department of Public Safety had investigated and ruled out homicides in two other jurisdictions.

To date, Angel had been charged with first-degree murder in connection with four slayings – two in Illinois, one in Kentucky and one in Texas. Cass County had filed the latest murder charge in connection with the killing of 87-year-old Leafie Mason in her Hughes Springs home.

The relatives of Resendez's most recent victims announced they were to seek more than $10 million in compensation for the authorities' errors.

New reports that Angel was now suspected of murdering up to 80 people came as little surprise to investigators. They'd always believed he must have killed many more than was currently known.

Investigators also chose the same moment to reveal for the first time that Angel used to sit down and make himself a meal in his victim's homes – after he'd bludgeoned them to death.

Devon Anderson, prosecutor in Harris County, Texas, explained, 'He takes his time. It appears that he enjoys hurting these people. In some cases he even helped himself to food after the killings.'

Shortly after the suspected serial killer's arrest, the Justice Department announced there would be a fuller inquiry into the circumstances behind the freeing of Angel Resendez from earlier INS custody on 2 June.

Some of Texas's most influential figures were furious about the way the alleged Railway Killer had eluded arrest for so long.

'This isn't just another serial killing. It's a catalogue of errors by authorities and a lot of heads are going to roll,' said Senator Lamar S Smith, before adding, 'It's just another example of the Immigration and Naturalization Service's complete lack of organisation.'

29

Outside the court, it was like a three-ring circus. An army of print, TV and radio journalists from all over the world were covering Texas's biggest news story since Waco. Every helicopter in Houston had been chartered and it was practically impossible to get within 30 feet of the court steps because of the media.

The carnival atmosphere surrounding Angel's first few court appearances must have sent out some conflicting messages to the alleged serial killer.

Like flies swarming over rotting meat, reporters and photographers swooped on anybody going in and out of the building, scribbling notes and snapping cameras at anything that moved.

Inside, the small bespectacled man, whom prosecutors claimed was the most dangerous serial killer seen in the US in recent years, bowed his head as he entered the court.

If the scene outside was theatrical, the one inside was

positively understated, with the man who slipped off and on trains with alarming ease to carry out his heinous crimes getting the sort of recognition he never really wanted.

Angel looked dazed and blankly continued staring at the floor as he stood before the judge on each occasion. He might have calmly walked across that border bridge and into the protective custody of the Texas Rangers, but it was already clear he would not be confessing to everything, as many had assumed.

All the speculation about a clever, devious criminal, a master of the art of disguise, a lingual genius – it all seemed to have paled into insignificance once Angel was captured. He simply did not live up to the image circulating when he was the most wanted man in America.

As one investigator pointed out, 'The guy acted like a nobody. It was so hard coming to terms with equating this quiet little fellow with the brutal crimes he was alleged to have committed.'

In some ways, Angel's physical appearance almost immediately turned him into a virtual antihero in the eyes of some. He fuelled a lot of people's imaginations by being so different from the stereotyped serial killers that we had become so used to seeing.

Here was a drifter, an apparent loser, possibly a repentant bad guy. The product of a dysfunctional home. By the time he'd reached adulthood and then endured all those horrific rapings and beatings in prison, he was looking for revenge.

Instead of taking it out on his family, he gradually developed into lashing out at anyone who got in the way of his criminal endeavours. Anyone whom he deemed to be a threat. Playing by his own violent rules led to his eventual capture. Could it really be that underneath the quiet, shy facade lurked a sick and twisted mind capable of the most appalling evil?

One of the FBI task force members summed up Angel this way: 'For millions, Angel provided a focus for fear and terror; while for others, mainly in his home country, he fulfilled a bizarre role of hero and madman, saint and outlaw.

'Here was a man who loved his mother until she betrayed him, deeply loved his wife and child. He protected all children and dogs. But he was also a man torn into shreds from the inside. A person who discarded opportunities and, in the rage that followed, became a serial killer.'

Meanwhile, the media frenzy surrounding Angel and his alleged crimes continued.

On the day of his court appearance on 14 July, hordes of satellite trucks were parked alongside the perimeter of the Harris County District Court.

When resident Maxiase Goldsberry, 39, learned what was happening. she needed no prodding to unleash an opinion. 'They ought to hang him – for all that killing he's been doing all over the states,' she said, her hand shading her eyes from the midday sun. 'Everybody can get some peace around here now,' she added.

On 15 July, Angel appeared once again in court in

Houston where he asked a judge, 'Can all this be done very quickly so I can say I'm guilty?'

The judge refused his request because under Texan law a defendant could not enter a plea until the trial started. It remained unclear whether Angel was trying to plead guilty to the burglary or murder charges against him.

Just before the case was adjourned, Angel beckoned his lawyers over to complain about his Bible being taken away from him and how he had been denied a kosher diet in jail.

~

So far, the authorities had confirmed that Resendez was being held directly responsible for nine murders. They are:

29 August 1997 – In Lexington, Kentucky, Christopher Maier, 21, was killed as he crossed railway tracks while going from one party to another.

17 December 1998 – In Houston, Texas, Dr Claudia Benton was found sexually assaulted, stabbed and beaten to death.

October 1998 – In Hughes Spring, Texas, 87-year-old Leafie Mason was attacked and killed by an intruder at her home next to a railway track.

2 May 1999 – In Weimar, Texas, Norman Sirnic and his wife Karen were found dead in their home.

Then after being released by immigration authorities:

4 June 1999 – In Fayette County, Texas, Josephine Konvicka, 73, found slain in her home.

5 June 1999 – In Houston, Texas, Noemi Dominguez found beaten to death in her home.

15 June 1999 – In Gorham, Illinois, George Morber and his daughter Carolyn Frederick found slain.

Behind the scenes, prosecutors in many of the cases against Angel were happy to sit back and await results of DNA evidence taken from the defendant after his surrender. It could be some weeks before all the murder charges were laid out in court.

~

The surge of worldwide publicity that surrounded the manhunt and capture of Angel Resendez ignored the plight of the communities left in a state of fear and terror by his murderous raids. After Claudia Benton's slaying in Houston, her husband and two daughters never returned to the house, and it was sold.

In the diminutive suburb of West University Place, where Dr Benton's brutally raped and repeatedly stabbed body was found, residents slowly began to regain their confidence once the suspect had surrendered.

The tragedy had in some ways brought many of the residents closer together. Other results of Angel Resendez's alleged actions were more obvious.

'We lock our front door now, more than we used to,' said one of Dr Benton's neighbours, Joyce Doyle, 50, as she and her husband and daughter prepared to take their dog out for an evening walk for the first time in more than six months.

On Lehigh Street, where Dr Benton lived, the blaring of locomotive horns still interrupted the cicadas whirring, but now that noise no longer sent a shiver of fear through many.

In the front gardens of almost every house on the block where Dr Benton lived were warnings of home-security systems or guard dogs. In the distance, the shimmering skyscrapers of downtown Houston seemed a million miles away. Not surprisingly home-security firms made a big sales push in the area following the killing.

Many neighbours in West University Place compiled a list of names and telephone numbers of each other and distributed it to all homeowners on the block. They had even met with the mayor and police to ask for more street lighting and signs to tell folks when they'd crossed the Houston city limits and entered West University Place.

As for the punishment for the accused murderer, Dr Benton's neighbours were surprisingly split on the issue. 'He should at least be kept in prison for the rest of his life. Maybe the death penalty. It depends,' said resident Joyce Doyle.

Another homeowner said, 'I feel he deserves justice. I don't believe in capital punishment, but I don't believe in parole either. And I don't believe he should get off on an insanity plea.'

~

Meanwhile, the INS embarrassment at releasing Angel

before he allegedly went on to kill four more people was further compounded whenever the screw-up was mentioned in the aftermath of the fugitive's surrender.

Yet, almost as soon as Angel Resendez gave himself up, INS officers in El Paso were trying to grab some of the credit for catching him on their turf. 'I don't know if it makes up for it, but there were some lessons that were learned,' commented Luis Garcia, District Director for the INS, parent agency of the border patrol.

CG Almengor, a supervisor at the border patrol processing facility where Angel was detained six weeks earlier, still claimed the agency's computer system did not indicate he was a wanted man. 'Our systems told us he was nothing of lookout material,' Almengor told reporters. 'We really wish he had been in the system so we could have caught him before.'

He didn't realise that this excuse had already been discounted in Washington.

~

Angel Resendez was told by his court-appointed lawyer that, if he was found guilty of capital murder in Texas, he could face death by lethal injection.

However, in the weeks following Angel's surrender, prosecutors decided not to reveal whether they would seek the death penalty or life imprisonment.

Ominously, Harris County, where Houston is located, is renowned for sending more prisoners to their deaths than any other US jurisdiction and, as the new millennium began had 143 people sitting on death row.

Only two years earlier – on 18 June 1997 – Texas had executed Irineo Tristan Montoya, a Mexican national convicted of killing a Houston cab driver. The case provoked furious protests from the Mexican consulate in Houston and citizens of Mexico.

There were 16 Mexican citizens on death row in Texas at that time, and negotiating Angel's surrender had been a remarkable achievement because the Mexican government habitually opposed the execution of its citizens. But neither Angel nor his attorney had contacted the local Mexican consulate for help. Although Houston's consul general Rodolfo Figueroa offered, 'If he does get in touch with the consulate, we will give him the same aid we afford other Mexicans in similar circumstances.'

That meant helping bring character witnesses to his trial, assistance with official documentation his lawyers might need, and a legal review of the case by an attorney employed by the consulate.

'We would want to make sure the defence is doing its job,' warned Figueroa.

But the capture of Angel Resendez did spell enormous relief for the Mexican community of Houston, even though many shared similar doubts about many aspects of the case. A lot of immigrants weren't convinced Angel had committed the crimes attributed to him. Others were angry at how lawmen had targeted many ordinary Mexicans during the multiple-agency manhunt for Angel. And there was a genuine fear that he could not possibly get a fair trial.

'Although it's a very large crime, it's not a good enough reason to kill him,' said Gilberto Castellano, 26, a Houston resident from the southern Mexican state of Michoacan. 'He should stay in jail. I think that's better.'

Others looked on it from another angle. Flavia Perez, a 44-year-old Mexico City resident, said, 'If he killed all those people, he should suffer. But, if they kill him, he won't suffer.'

Some Mexicans believed that law-enforcement agencies used the high-profile nature of the manhunt for Angel as an excuse to look for illegal aliens.

'The police are taking advantage of this opportunity to persecute them,' said Dora Alicia Del Bosque. 'They're not just asking for their identification, but their documentation as well.'

Mexicans in Houston had paid close attention to the manhunt because many enquiries had been made within their community at the time.

Joel Mendoza, a 31-year-old electrician from Mexico City who had lived in Houston for four years, said he was angry at Angel as well as at overzealous US law-enforcement agents. 'I feel ashamed that he's Mexican,' said Mendoza, pausing between bites of a breakfast taco at an outdoor food stand in downtown Houston. 'Because of him, a bunch of my people get stopped when they come into the United States just because he messed up.'

But Mendoza and many other Mexicans were equally angry that the press had been so quick to condemn Angel before he had even entered a formal plea against the charges, let alone be tried or found guilty.

However, he did concede, 'If he's guilty, let's kill him. No mercy.'

30

The Railway Killer case took a new turn in the middle of July when investigators decided not to reveal any more about their enquiries following Angel's capture. In Houston, officials refused to say if DNA taken from the suspected serial killer matched samples found in the home of slain doctor Claudia Benton.

It was clear that investigators feared Angel Resendez would plead not guilty and much of their painstakingly gathered evidence might prove crucial to proving he was the man responsible for a murder spree.

On 16 July, police investigators from Lexington, Kentucky, were allowed to interview Angel about the slaying of student Christopher Maier and the rape of his girlfriend.

Within an hour, Sergeant Mike Barnard emerged from the Harris County Jail with a look of steely satisfaction on his face. 'He's our man,' said Barnard. 'And he knows we know. There's no doubt in our mind.'

That same day, Lexington prosecutor Ray Larson met up with his counterpart from Illinois in an office at the FBI field offices in Houston. They wanted to jointly create a plan that would guarantee bringing Angel to justice for the murders he was alleged to have committed outside Texas.

However, one Texas prosecutor told news media later that evening there was no point 'because he's gonna fry here anyhow'.

Investigator Mike Barnard wasn't so sure. He told a press conference in Houston, 'Texas has him, but that doesn't mean they'll prosecute him first.'

~

But it was the haunting spectre of death row that most disturbed Angel Resendez and his legal team.

As the prison population throughout the US soared by the rate of more than 70,000 a year, so did the number of prisoners on death row – the terrifying purgatory where death is only a short walk away.

Despite campaigns across the country, America remains hell-bent on exacting revenge on the bad guys. Just putting them in jail and throwing away the key is not enough. US citizens demand 'an eye for an eye'.

In 1980, only 500 men and five women were awaiting execution in the US. At the end of 1999, that number had jumped to more than 3,000. Since 1976, 300 executions have taken place. But a lot more lie ahead.

What concerned Angel and his court-appointed lawyers was that not only might he be sentenced to death but also that he would then face the agonising wait on death row, a prison within a prison, a segregated section for the baddest of the bad in a state where executions are as familiar as snakes on the prairie, that can often stretch into 10 or even 15 years. Death-row inmates live in a world that is for the most part dank, airless and devoid of sunlight.

Angel feared he would spend his life living within spitting distance of the gas chamber, the electric chair or an antiseptic hospital-like room where lethal injections are administered with machine-like efficiency. But the public perception of death row as being a place where psychopaths, lunatics and mental defectives foam at the mouth as they hang off their cell bars is far from accurate.

~

On 24 July 1999, a grand jury indicted Angel Resendez on a capital murder charge for the slaying of Houston physician Claudia Benton.

Prosecutors openly admitted they had not yet decided for certain whether they would be seeking the death penalty. Arraignment for the charge was set for the following day.

The grand jury returned the indictment after 45 minutes of presentations by prosecutors who produced fingerprints and other evidence to link Angel to the slaying of Dr Benton.

Assistant District Attorney Devon Anderson said it would be another month before any decision was made on the death penalty issue. But, when asked if there was any way this was not a death penalty case, she replied, 'No.'

Anderson told the court that Angel would undergo a psychiatric evaluation to determine whether he was competent to stand trial. 'The next step is to gather our punishment evidence... to decide whether we're seeking the death penalty or not.'

Meanwhile, Angel remained in custody without bond. Lawyers told the court they had found one of his fingerprints in Benton's stolen Jeep and referred to the jewellery associated with her that was found at his home in Rodeo.

Officials at the court also mentioned that there was similar evidence linking Angel with the June slaying of Houston schoolteacher Noemi Dominguez.

Representatives of three authorities in Texas where other victims were allegedly slain by the suspect agreed to let the Benton case move forward before pursuing their own cases.

31

Within weeks of his incarceration at Harris County Jail, Angel Resendez discovered that there were dozens of women throughout America who actually believed that the best men are in prison.

Despite the horrific details beginning to emerge about his alleged crimes, a number of letters from such women turned up at the jail following Angel's dramatic surrender.

For, in the US in 1999, a growing number of women were looking to jails and prisons – even death row – for lovers and husbands.

Most of these women knew only too well they would never even spend a single night of intimacy with their incarcerated boyfriend or husband. But that didn't seem to matter.

The letters that arrived for Angel requested that he become a penpal. In prisons across the US, it's not unusual for a convict to be corresponding with as many as 30 women at the same time.

But Angel had only just been arrested.

His criminal 'hero' and namesake Night Stalker Richard Ramirez had, over the years, attracted vast numbers of admiring women. And, on 27 June 1996, he even married one such women in a ceremony inside San Quentin.

Back in Harris County Jail, officials were astounded by the 'fan mail' Angel was receiving. Much of it was from Latina women, and some speculated that the Satanic messages that Angel was alleged to have daubed on the walls at the scene of some of the slayings had also caught the attention of many women.

But, as one task force investigator pointed out, 'Why in the world would a normally intelligent woman look to someone like Angel Resendez for that special man she wishes to share her life with?'

Many experts who have studied the phenomenon of prison groupies say that the guilt and innocence of a convict is irrelevant. They believe that most of these women suffer from low self-esteem, a need to control others, and Florence Nightingale or saviour complexes. Some even find the idea of a man in prison appeals to their sadomasochistic instincts.

One psychiatrist described prison groupies as often being the type who adopt stray puppies. They have a pathological or abnormal need to assist or help someone else.

Often the woman in question is someone who hasn't

been able to form significant relationships in her own life, or they have tremendous feelings of guilt about something they believe they have done in the past and must expiate.

Many of these women see themselves as saviours, whose love will help salvage a bad man. They feel their love for an individual, whom the rest of society has given up on or abhors, gives them personal validation and worth.

'But these women are playing with fire,' says one expert.

The most horrific example of this came in California when a 19-year-old school clerk was abducted and raped after initiating an ill-conceived pen-pal relationship with a stick-up man serving time at San Bernardino County's Prado Conservation Camp next to the more secure California Institution for Men in Chino.

Eighteen months after starting the correspondence, the armed robber escaped and, with the help of a female associate, kidnapped the girl he'd been writing to and took her to a motel room. There she was raped and forced to perform oral sex, then tied to a bed with torn sheets. After enduring a harrowing night of repeated sexual abuse, she escaped when her abductor injected himself with heroin and dozed off.

In Kentucky, law-enforcement investigators were resigned to the fact that they might never actually try Angel for the murder of Christopher Maier in Lexington two years earlier because of the trials he faced in other states first.

32

Back in 1989, lawyers representing notorious LA serial Killer Richard 'Night Stalker' Ramirez employed every legal angle available to them to convince the trial jury that their client was innocent.

But the man who Angel Resendez so avidly read about when he was in prison in Florida had sealed his own fate the moment he admitted to an arresting officer when he was finally captured, 'Yeah, man, I'm Richard Ramirez... I did it, you know. You guys got me, the Stalker.'

It seems unlikely Resendez said anything similar to Texas Ranger Drew Carter.

Resendez's trial would to a certain extent rest upon the testimony of mental-health specialists, who would try to explain his personal history and mental instability. Having met with Resendez in the run-up to the trial, they would refer to his apparent alcoholism;

his lack of an early education, and the trauma of that sexual attack by older boys.

They also discussed conditions such as cortical dysfunction – something that is not apparent when meeting someone on the street but becomes clear after a battery of tests have been run on the patient.

The results of other medical and educational tests taken throughout Resendez's life would also be produced in order to back up claims of some level of borderline personality disorder.

To many experts, Resendez was a classic example. He met all eight criteria as established by the *Diagnostic and Statistical Manual of Mental Disorders* – a standard reference used by clinicians in determining psychological dysfunctions. It defines the borderline as 'a personality disorder in which there is instability in a variety of areas, including interpersonal behaviour, mood and self-image. No single feature is invariably present.'

The disorder is actually more commonly diagnosed in women, but it is prevalent throughout the clinical population and is associated with the better-known antisocial personality disorder. Only five of the eight criteria are needed for a diagnosis. Resendez scored well above that.

~

1. Impulsivity or unpredictability in at least two areas that are self-damaging – spending, sex, gambling, substance abuse, shoplifting, overeating, physically self-damaging acts.

2. A pattern of unstable and intense interpersonal relationships – marked shifts of attitude, idealisation, devaluation, manipulation.
3. Inappropriate, intense anger or lack of control of anger.
4. Identity disturbance, manifested by uncertainty about... self-image, gender identification, long-term goals, friendship patterns, values, loyalties.
5. Affective instability – marked shifts from normal mood to depression, irritability or anxiety, usually lasting only a few hours and only rarely a few days, with a return to a normal mood.
6. Intolerance of being alone, frantic efforts to avoid being alone, depressed when alone.
7. Physically self-damaging acts, suicidal gestures, self-mutilation, recurrent accidents or physical fights.
8. Chronic feelings of emptiness or boredom.

~

Not surprisingly, the antisocial personality diagnosis would fit most of the prison population of the United States. But there seems little doubt that such expert testimony would take up many hours of the trial.

No doubt the prosecution would also claim that mental impairment was the last resort in defence terms. They would insist that in the eyes of the law it was not whether Resendez was manipulative and perverted – but whether he *knew* what he was doing and that what he was doing was wrong. His mental impairment would hinge upon expert testimony and that of Angel's friends and family.

But then who would be responsible for the deaths of at least nine people?

Resendez's team would say it was genetics. They'd blame it on his absent father and overbearing mother. He blamed the detectives. He also blamed his victims.

Others expected to give evidence included Resendez's friends and relatives when it came to the penalty phase of the trial.

But the most important witness of all remained the girlfriend of Resendez's first alleged victim, Lexington student Christopher Maier. If the defence attorney decided he had to plead not guilty, then she could expect to be put through the appalling pain and anguish of reliving that horrific night back in August 1997.

No doubt, a jury response to such an awful ordeal would have a large bearing on whether she was in fact called to the witness stand.

But then if the prosecutors had all the forensic evidence they said they had then it would seem that no amount of personal testimony would prevent a jury from finding Resendez guilty and sending him to death row.

EPILOGUE

Not long after Resendez's arrest, former Texas Attorney General Jim Mattox – wary of the controversy miring the many confessions and recantations of other notorious serial killers such as Henry Lee Lucas – remarked, 'I hope they don't start pinning on him every crime that happens near a railway track.'

However, it became clear that Resendez was responsible for many more killings than was at first thought.

In Houston, Resendez eventually dropped a request to have his murder trial moved to another city. Earlier, he'd claimed he did not want to risk facing a jury composed of 'rednecks and Germans'. After extensive discussions with his state-appointed attorneys, he decided to accept the location.

On 18 May 2000, Resendez was found guilty of capital murder for the 1998 rape and murder of

Houston-area doctor Claudia Benton after he had, as expected, pleaded not guilty by reason of insanity. The Houston jury of six men and six women deliberated ten hours over two days before reaching its unanimous verdict and would next decide whether Resendez, now 40, should go to prison for life or die by lethal injection.

Resendez's attorney admitted at the trial's opening that he'd murdered nine people during a two-year US killing spree in Texas, Illinois and Kentucky.

Two weeks later, Resendez was sentenced to death for the murder of Dr Benton. A psychiatrist hired by the defence testified that Resendez was a paranoid schizophrenic, who believed he was an avenging angel directed by God to kill evil people.

But prosecutors said he was simply a murderer feigning insanity to cover his crimes. Resendez was told he would die by lethal injection.

'I don't believe in death,' Resendez told The Associated Press in 2000, shortly after arriving on death row. 'I know the body is going to go to waste. But me, as a person, I'm eternal. I'm going to be alive forever.'

~

In 2002, Resendez wrote a letter to a central Florida sheriff admitting killing two teens in his district in 1997 and gave details about the slayings that investigators said no one but the killer and investigators would know.

'We cannot say 100 per cent he did it,' explained Major Patti Lumpkin, supervisor of the Marion County Sheriff's Major Crimes Unit. 'Until we have all the facts, and interview Resendez in person, we just cannot say right now. We do not want to pin a murder on him just because he has been convicted of another.'

Resendez said in his letter that the killings occurred on the railway tracks between Tampa and Baldwin, 20 miles east of Jacksonville, Florida. The tracks run through Belleview, where 19-year-old Jesse Howell was found slain on 23 March 1997. His 16-year-old travelling companion, Wendy VonHuben, was never found.

Investigators had never made public what type of weapon was used to fatally beat Howell, but Resendez correctly identified the weapon in his letter, according to local law-enforcement officials. They also said Resendez provided two maps in his letter that showed where he said he killed the man and buried the girl.

The day before Howell was killed, Resendez was issued with a trespass warning by railway officials at a switching station 90 miles north of the location where he said he'd killed the pair. Further later evidence confirmed Resendez's claims and law-enforcement officials then closed the case.

On Wednesday, 12 April 2006, the San Antonio Police Department, in Texas, announced it had cleared up the unsolved murder of Michael White, who was found shot to death in July 1991 in the front garden of a vacant house in downtown San Antonio. According to San Antonio Police, Angel Resendez gave them precise details about that murder as well, and he was then named as the perpetrator.

~

A few weeks before he was due to be put to death, the Mexican government announced plans to fight Resendez's execution on the grounds that he was mentally unstable. Foreign Relations Secretary Luis Ernesto Derbez sent a letter to the Texas parole board opposing the Resendez's execution by lethal injection.

But on 21 June 2006, a Houston judge ruled that Resendez was mentally competent to be executed and the Mexican government dropped their appeal. The judge rejected Resendez's lawyers claims that mental delusions made him ineligible for execution. He was set to be the 13th inmate executed that year in Texas. Upon hearing the judge's ruling, Resendez simply repeated what he'd said earlier: 'I'm eternal. I'm going to be alive forever.' He also continued to describe himself as half-man and half-angel and reassured psychiatrists he couldn't be executed because he didn't believe he could die.

These bizarre statements led psychiatric specialists to believe that perhaps Resendez was, in fact, not competent to be executed. In the words of one psychiatrist who had twice evaluated Resendez in 2006, 'Delusions had completely taken over Resendez's thought processes.'

However, Resendez was told his execution on 27 June by lethal injection for the murder of Dr Claudia Benton would go ahead, despite an appeal pending with the 5th US Circuit Court of Appeals.

Resendez was taken into the death chamber at Huntsville Penitentiary, Texas, at just before 8 pm on

27 June 2006. In his final statement, Resendez said he deserved what he was getting and asked for forgiveness. Resendez then mumbled a prayer, saying, 'Lord, forgive me. Lord, forgive me,' as he waited for the lethal injection to proceed. His feet nervously tapped a white sheet partially covering him. He acknowledged the presence of relatives watching through a nearby window and then turned and looked towards the relatives of his victims in another room.

'I want to ask if it is in your heart to forgive me,' he said in English, looking towards relatives of some of his victims. 'You don't have to. I know I allowed the devil to rule my life. I just ask you to forgive me and ask the Lord to forgive me for allowing the devil to deceive me.'

He then added his now favourite phrase: 'I'm eternal. I'm going to be alive forever.'

George Benton, the husband of victim Dr Claudia Benton, who was present at the execution dismissed Resendez's remorse, describing him as 'evil contained in human form, a creature without a soul, no conscience, no sense of remorse, no regard for the sanctity of human life'.

Resendez was pronounced dead at 8.05 pm central time (905 ET).

~

When Resendez had surrendered to the Texas Rangers on that border bridge near El Paso, it wasn't exactly the actions of a deadly, determined serial killer. Indeed, many who have considered his past record, in contrast to the profile generated from the crime scenes, now believe that Resendez doesn't truly fit the profile of the so-called Railway Killer.

'I have doubts about this guy,' one highly experienced psychiatrist told this author. 'I'd need to see more examples of his powers of organisation, deliberation, calculation. Something that shows me he planned all this carefully. There has to be a flash of criminal genius – call it brilliance, if you want, but all serial killers have it.'

However, there are aspects of Resendez's relationship with his mother, Virginia, that point to some of the more obvious conclusions. 'What interested me was the way that he was such a mommy's boy and then he was rejected, so he ran away at an incredibly early age,' says the same psychologist.

'There was definitely a level of choosing done in each murder scene, even though he didn't plan any of them ahead of time. It was as if many of his victims represented his mom.'

But, unlike most serial killers, there was no real attempt to boast about the killings by arranging the victims in a grotesque manner.

'Often that is done to shock and upset the police or whoever has to deal with the bodies. It's an expression of rage that you feel towards authority. But this guy didn't do that. It was almost as if he was ashamed of what he'd done.'

It's standard operating procedure for the friends and family of a serial killer to express disbelief in a person's guilt. How could someone they thought they knew so well be responsible for such heinous crimes? It's always disconcerting for those who knew that individual in a non-violent context to come to terms with the fact that a so-called regular guy was actually a monster capable of the worst atrocities.

Cops and crime investigators know only too well how ordinary lawbreakers can be, but they like to think they can always size a person up. What disconcerted so many detectives about Angel Resendez was that he was known to many as a habitual small-time offender, with an MO as an illegal immigrant who liked to burgle people's homes and steal their cars.

It's highly likely that Angel committed many more crimes than have been reported here, but he wasn't exactly a successful career criminal. He'd been caught many times. It was almost as if the burglaries and other minor offences were an invitation to be arrested. Of course, he always made an effort to get away, but he didn't try that hard and whenever he was apprehended he'd roll over and give up immediately.

On the other hand, the Railway Killer had obviously gone to greater lengths to ensure that he got away with murder by slaughtering anyone who witnessed his intrusion into their homes.

So there we have it. An enigmatic, shadowy killer who's gone to his grave with a thousand secrets still unsolved.

Postscript

There are no markers or monuments on the railway tracks near Rosemont Garden and Suburban Court in Lexington, Kentucky. No wooden crosses or replenished bunches of flowers as there so often are at the scenes of car crashes.

The only thing that stands out among the weeds and wildflowers is a cedar tree rising about three feet out of the soil.

It sways every time the freight trains shunt slowly through Lexington as a lasting reminder of the spot where Angel Resendez's first alleged victim, student Christopher Maier, was so brutally slain.

It was a killing that was the first of a terrifying series of murders that sparked a manhunt that swept the entire nation in a tide of fear. From that moment on, every time the blast of the trains was heard, it sent a shiver through the residents of that densely populated area on the edge of town. Was the Railway Killer about to strike again?

Dying don't scare me. I'll be in hell. With Satan. Gotta be a better fucking place than this.

– **Richard Ramirez,** the so-called Night Stalker
serial killer who murdered 13 people in
Los Angeles in the mid-1980s

About the Author

Wensley Clarkson has written 30 books, which have sold over a million copies in more than a dozen countries worldwide, including 15 bestselling true-crime books. Some of those titles are *Doctors of Death*, *Whatever Mother Says*, *Deadly Seduction*, *Slave Girls* and *Caged Heat*. He divides his time between homes in London, Los Angeles and Spain.